Endorsements for *The Things We Live With*

The Things We Live With is a tender cartography of grief and familial legacy, in which Gemma Nisbet elegantly explores how the maps we make—whether by story, memory, art, or artefact—inevitably fall shy of the territory.

Josephine Rowe

What are we to make of all these things around us? And what are they to make of us? Delicately, as if unpacking a box of fragile treasures, Nisbit cups in her hands and presents us with a series of relationships: with old, loved things, with her family, and her own crushable centre. They are all, it turns out, well kept in the same box. Nisbit wraps her meditations in soft words and firm intelligence, and in this wonderful, digressive and intently considered work she uncovers the tender meaning of possessions, and what it is to be possessed by them too. As a devoted keeper of objects, I read this book with recognition and envy, and anyone who inherits, hoards, abhors or adores the relics of their lives will appreciate Nisbit's candour and contemplations.

Kate Holden

Wise, profound and with tender humour *The Things We Live With* expands our thinking about the power of objects to shape our sense of self, anchor our memories, and reflect our place in the world. In these superb, engrossing essays Gemma Nisbet draws us in close as she examines what we hold onto, what we let go, and the complex relationships between the tangible and intangible. A moving portrayal of grief, love, and legacy, this is a collection to treasure.

Vanessa Berry

The Things
We Live With

Gemma Nisbet

Gemma Nisbet is a Western Australian-based writer whose work has appeared in *Westerly*, *Australian Book Review* and *TEXT*, among other publications. A former travel journalist, she recently completed a PhD in Creative Writing at the University of Western Australia, teaches Creative Writing and Literary Studies at universities, and writes a weekly book reviews and interviews column for *The West Australian*. She lives on Whadjuk Noongar Boodja with her husband and their dog, Pickle.

The Things We Live With is her first book.

Gemma Nisbet

The Things We Live With

Essays on Uncertainty

First published in Australia in 2023
by Upswell Publishing
Perth, Western Australia
upswellpublishing.com

ISBN: 978-0-645-53680-5

 A catalogue record for this
book is available from the
National Library of Australia

Cover design by Chil3, Fremantle
Typeset in Foundry Origin by Lasertype

Upswell Publishing is assisted by the State of Western Australia
through its funding program for arts and culture.

Department of
**Local Government, Sport
and Cultural Industries**

Contents

Edward Sylvester Hynes 9

Baby Teeth 23

The Things We Live With, Part I 37

A Small, Brown Suitcase 51

Dear Lucy 65

The Things We Live With, Part II 79

On We Go 93

Via del Paradiso 105

Swimming, or Hoping 121

Coda 145

Notes on sources 157

Acknowledgements 163

Edward Sylvester Hynes

Seeing him was like spotting a familiar face in a crowd of strangers. A man, grinning broadly, his nose bulbous, Adam's apple prominent, eyes the colour of the ocean on a February morning. He had dark, bushy brows, long sideburns and a five o'clock shadow. I'd known his face for as long as I could remember. My dad had hauled that painting—a portrait in oils, about the size of an A3 sheet of paper, framed in cheap wood painted gold—from house to house each time we'd moved. Of course he'd taken it when he and my mother had divorced. Of course he'd taken it when he and my stepmum returned to England. The picture was as ugly as I'd recalled, and seeing it felt like being reunited with an old friend.

That's how it was during that cluster of days at my stepmum's house in England when we sorted through my dad's possessions: those shocks of recognition punctuating the drawn-out decisions over what to keep and what to consign to the charity shop in the next village. I quickly found that it was easy to decide to hang on to things: the intricate marquetry pictures Dad had made in his immaculately organised shed, the book of poetry he'd had since his schooldays. The painting of the man, of course. But letting things go was more fraught. The books he'd never mentioned, the ephemera I had no recollection of, the old papers that distinguished themselves only by bearing his handwriting. The photos were especially difficult, evoking family meals and holidays, some of which I'd forgotten until I saw them fixed in faded colour.

I had not anticipated the way grief could so quickly become an intimate encounter with stuff. Not just the matter—the ashes, the remains—that your loved one becomes, but also the things they leave behind. Their possessions, mundane and precious, suddenly transform into treasured relics, and even the most trivial items are overlaid with a special significance born of loss; a newfound capacity to resist your best efforts at insisting they are just *objects*.

Still, there wasn't room in my luggage to take it all home. So eventually I popped certificates out of frames and pictures into envelopes and swaddled the painting in clothing, laying it carefully across the top of my suitcase to be carried all the way back to Australia. I was worried it would crack or snap in transit, but it emerged at the other end intact and unscathed.

This is how I became interested in things. In their strange pull and power, in the ways they hold on to us and we to them.

o o o

I've wondered, over the years, about that portrait I hauled home from England: who painted it, where it came from, why it hung in pride of place in every home my parents and I had lived in together. I once tried to figure it out, but the avenues for enquiry were limited. I recalled my mum telling me only that Dad had bought the painting before they'd met. I googled the name signed in the bottom left-hand corner of the picture—'E Hynes'—but it was sufficiently generic that my search turned up nothing useful.

I knew little for sure about the painting and its provenance, but I'd always imagined the man it depicted was someone like my dad. He wore a beaten-up hat, and worn-out clothes. A well-earned pint was clasped in one huge hand, a pipe in the other. His rosy cheeks suggested an outdoor life, and he looked like someone who could set a camp and cook over an open fire, read a map and tie knots.

He reminded me, too, of the Bush Tucker Man, who I'd watched on television as a child, cruising around in his Land Rover, his distinctively modified Akubra hat casting a deep shade over his face as he was guided in collecting bush foods by Aboriginal women in billowing dresses and catching mud crabs by elderly men with faces etched like topographical maps.

The Bush Tucker Man also reminded me of my dad. But where his show's twangy theme tune signalled another instalment of his adventures cataloguing native fruits and traditional knowledge on behalf of the Australian army, my dad headed bush with a more straightforwardly extractive mission, in search of minerals, mainly copper and gold. An exploration geologist—a one-time winner of the Prospector of the Year award, no less—he would return bearing hunks of rock with metallic flecks or smooth cylinders he called core samples.

To me, when I was a child, the Bush Tucker Man, my dad and the painting seemed so much alike as to be almost the same person. Like the former, my dad had a hat and a truck. He had the same hairy legs poking out of a very similar pair of well-worn shorts, the same toothy smile and traces of the same north Queensland accent that turns 'beauty' into 'bewdy' and 'cool' into 'kewl'. They were about the same age, and shared some idioms, even some mannerisms: an economical way of speaking out of a corner of the mouth as if to keep flies out; a slouchy self-possession. Most of all, they had that habit of squinting, as if staring into the sun, in photographs.

I have a photo somewhere of Dad making that face as a little kid, standing in the dirt against a chain-link fence. Despite the fact that the body supposedly replaces itself entirely every ten years as old cells die and are renewed—making each of us entirely new, physically speaking, every decade or so—I can already see the adult my dad would become in the boy in this photograph. The long limbs, and the baby-soft hair slicked to one side; but most of all, that expression and those eyes, looking askance at the camera.

○ ○ ○

Once, when he got back from a work trip, he gave you a rectangle of rock, its reddish face speckled white and grey and pink, with the lightest dusting of gold. It has always seemed unbearably precious, even after you realised it probably isn't worth much.

Something about those flecks of gold makes you think, now, of the cluster of abnormal cells—multiplying, uncontrolled—at the back of his eye. Ocular melanoma is a very rare cancer (something like five cases per million people). But, when you google it, you learn that gold is even rarer (around three parts per billion in the Earth's crust).

One of the things you learnt about gold in high-school chemistry is that it is a 'noble' element: inert and largely chemically unreactive. This is one of the reasons it is so useful to humans; why we have so diligently sought it out for so many thousands of years. This must be, you think, one of the reasons they use it in one of the treatments for eye cancers, in which a small disk that looks a lot like a bottle cap is lined with radioactive material and inserted near the tumour to kill the malignant cells. Most usually, this disk is made from gold.

It was too late for any of that by the time his condition was identified. It is difficult to diagnose eye cancers, because by the time they make themselves known—sometimes with a dark spot reaching like a shadow across the iris—they've often already metastasised, having spread unchecked throughout the body.

○ ○ ○

It must have been a couple of years after I got home from that trip to see my stepmum that one of my dad's close friends pulled up outside my house. From the backseat of his car, he retrieved two heavy boxes of papers and files. Later, I had a cursory sort through the typed sheets and handwritten notes, all connected to Dad's PhD research on the rock formations of a specific part of east-central Vermont. But the boxes mostly just sat on the floor in the room where I work, until I found a spot to store them in the attic, where they've sat ever since.

Those boxes were just a few drops in a slow-seeping stream of stuff that had begun to flow after I'd returned from England, bringing forth objects unearthed in spare-room closets and at the back of cluttered cupboards by family members and my dad's friends and former colleagues. I'd quickly come to see that accepting them would be a kindness, allowing people to pass on items that sentimentality prevented them from discarding outright. I understood the impulse; how throwing these objects away would feel like putting a piece of my father into the bin.

Or maybe it was just a convenient excuse, this air of altruism, for I soon became greedy for these things. I thus acquired Dad's favourite Brisbane Broncos t-shirt and his parents' wedding rings. I collected the fleecy black cap with earflaps that he wore when working somewhere cold, his faded khaki fishing vest, and his Akubra hat. I stashed away the pictures from the day he married my mum, and even a slim envelope of love letters he had written to her.

Philosopher and theorist Jane Bennett has spoken about how hoarding is often represented 'as a coping response to human mortality', to 'the death of a parent, child or marriage or an empty nest'. 'The hoarder,' she says, 'desperately clings to things because metal, plastic, ceramic, glass [and] wood last longer than human flesh, so the relatively slow rate of decay of those things might present the reassuring illusion that at least something doesn't die.'

The difference between my behaviour and compulsive hoarding is akin to the distance between passing sadness and depression, and I don't wish to minimise the suffering it entails. But I see something of myself in Bennett's description of the way a hoard of stuff 'can provide a veritable cocoon' in which the 'slowness' of these objects—their ability to endure over time—'is preferred to the faster and more visible rate of decay that characterises human bodies' and relationships.

I thought that all those objects connected to my dad's life would act as inert and immutable vessels into which I could pour memories—mine, and other people's—for safe storage. In much the same way that the Bush Tucker Man or my dad might have used a compass to find their way or a jack to change a tyre, I figured I could make use of this stuff like a tool, as a buttress to memory, a reef that might shore up the island against the twinned tides of forgetfulness and time.

o o o

One of the things I liked about the Bush Tucker Man as a child was the way he always seemed to be in possession of exactly what he needed and little more. He was neither under nor overprepared, his shovel and winch bolted to the bonnet and bull bar of his truck, his backpack ready to be swung from the tray to his shoulder at a moment's notice. Some of my favourite scenes showed him casually fixing a busted water canister with a nugget of plant resin or building a makeshift yabby trap out of a hollowed-out tree trunk and a bit of string, like some lanky-legged Aussie MacGyver, his eyes a mineral seam sparkling in the shadow of his broad-brimmed hat.

And though my dad kept his tools on a precisely organised pegboard in his shed—the outline of each hammer and wrench traced in black marker—rather than bolted to the bonnet of his truck, I imagined that he, too, would never be caught unprepared. He was a person who could change a tyre and light a campfire, catch a fish and reverse a trailer. This highly organised approach extended to other areas of his life. I remember standing, quite transfixed, in front of the elaborately colour-coded wall planner that hung in his office, and admiring the methodically arranged contents of the tackle box he took fishing, in which each hook and lure was slotted into its correct compartment.

Then there was his steady adherence to arriving home at 6.30 on the dot each evening. The way we rarely heard from him when he was away working. How he seemed able to compartmentalise his inner life, and spoke so infrequently to me about his past, as if his memories were a collection of objects he could pick up from a shelf to admire as required before neatly putting them away once again.

I have learnt, since my dad died, that it is a burden to attempt to always appear capable, to give the impression you are in control all the time. That endeavouring to do so can exact a heavy toll on a person. That the Bush Tucker Man could seem—at least to my prepubescent self—to achieve such a feat came down in part, no doubt, to the benign trickery of television. He could do a second, or a third, take of a scene, and then walk off screen and become the person he was in real life. The rest of us have only one chance to get it right.

o o o

The two of you never spoke about how depression felt to him, but for you it has occasionally included the sensation of feeling detached or disconnected from your body, like you are watching yourself from the outside. As if you can suddenly see all the ways that everyone else views you even as you retain an awareness that it is just a projection, a trick of an over-anxious mind.

This fragmentation of self-perception has always been, for you, a mercifully fleeting sensation, a cloud passing quickly across the sun. But you have read that this dissociation is something people often find difficult to express, employing simile and metaphor as they attempt to describe something that resists being rendered in words. It feels like being a robot, they might say. As if you are seeing your life through a pane of glass, through a thick fog, or in a film.

This, too, is how you've often felt that you're seeing him: through a low mist, or a dirty window, squinting. The philosopher Max Black described metaphors in a similar way: as a visual filter; a piece of smoked glass through which you might look at the thing you are trying to describe, the opaque sections of the glass casting some associations into shadow while, by default, drawing attention to the ones that remain visible. As tools that can capture the essence of something more fully than straightforward description, but which can also obscure and mislead.

It took you a long time to realise that the ways in which you understood your dad—using the Bush Tucker Man or the painting of the bushman—might have a similar effect. That they might quietly be making a case for who he had been and how you have recollected him even as they cast other portions of his person into shade.

o o o

At some points since my dad died, it has seemed as though my whole house was filled with objects connected to him. His old compass and the deeply silly ceramic figurine of a rat sandwiched between two slices of bread perched on a shelf in my office. In the kitchen, the family crest with the tartan and the wild boar and the Gaelic motto that translates to 'I endure'. The room with the piano has his books of sheet music with their orderly pencil notations; the bedroom his watch, which I altered to fit my wrist but never wear. Even the laundry, the bathroom, have their souvenirs: the lace tablecloth his mother made, folded among the clean sheets; the wooden brush whose bristles, I fancy, still contain some strands of his fine, brown hair.

Then there are the images: the real ones and those that exist in my mind. The painting, and the photographs. He and my mum, when he still had that moustache. He and my stepmum at their wedding. Him, holding me when I was a baby, his hand as big as my whole body. Crouched by a granite boulder. Standing by a lake, a slender fishing rod under one arm. Playing Chopin on the piano, or doing that trick where he popped the top off a stubby with the underside of his brow.

It has been difficult, sometimes, to keep all of these pictures straight, whether in their boxes or in my head. No one is ever one thing, even when they're alive, but sometimes it has felt as if the person my father was has shattered into as many pieces as there are individual memories and related objects; that remembering him has required sweeping up the shards and trying to put them back together. It's been like assembling a jigsaw puzzle, but with only a snatched recollection—ever-decaying, ever-changeable—as a guide to how the finished picture should look. Of course, some of the pieces of the puzzle have gone missing, too, meaning those that remain risk taking on an outsize importance through the sheer force of their presence. I am deeply sceptical of the idea that hanging on to stuff that reminds us of the past is inherently pathological and that freeing ourselves from possessions is a sure-fire way to escape unhealthy patterns of thought and behaviour. And yet I'll admit that it has sometimes felt as if there were too many of these objects, too many of these memories, for me to make sense of them all.

I had assumed the objects I have amassed would possess an endless capacity to evoke the past. And yet, when I pick up that rock he gave me—the one with the glint of gold on one faceted face—I cannot recall the significance of the others that sit alongside it. There's a pale stone, its surface worn smooth by water. A flat piece of quartz with a thin, dark vein. A rough lump shot with sparkly flakes of what I think might be mica. He must have given me at least some of them, but beyond that, the imagined storehouse of memory is bare.

Instead, they serve as reminders of the precious things that have faded, despite my best efforts: among them, my ability to recall with any certainty the precise blue of my dad's eyes and the sound of his voice on the phone. If his possessions have been a way for me to try to hold other things together, then they have also become a barometer of the ways my memories of him have begun, inexorably, to crumble.

They remind me, too, that there is not an infinite number of objects connected with my dad's life, and that the flow of his possessions into my home has gradually tapered off since he died. It has now been a long time since anyone has given me an item related to him. If anything, in recent times it has been me who has actively pursued them, seeking out the ever-more esoteric. Most recently, I submitted a form to the hospital where he died requesting a copy of his medical records.

All I could think to write under the section asking for my reason for doing so was 'personal interest'.

o o o

You recall, as a child, attempting to imitate some of the feats of quiet competence you saw your dad and the Bush Tucker Man executing. You, too, wanted to be able to set a camp and read a map and tie knots. To change a tyre and light a campfire, catch a fish and reverse a trailer. You never had much success with any of that. But more recently, you've wondered what else you might have learnt to emulate from these seemingly self-contained men, with their capacity for creating the illusion of control. Whether that might also be one of your father's legacies.

You've wondered, too, about the bushman: about the archetype that lurks in the background of the painting on your wall. You notice that if you look at him one way, he's smiling, jovial, a hard worker, a mate. Look at him from another perspective and he might appear looming and leery, his laughter sinister, sneering. Look at him from another and you might see a threat, implicit or otherwise, in his large hands and corporeal bulk; might notice that his smile never quite reaches his eyes. You might wonder about who gets to be called a bushman, who doesn't, and why.

You've also thought of the scars that peppered your dad's arms and shoulders. He was always having dodgy moles cut out and, for a long time, you'd assumed that his cancer must have been caused by so much time spent outside due, in large part, to his work. But then you read that researchers aren't certain there's a link between sun exposure and ocular melanoma. What exactly causes the cells to mutate into tumours remains difficult to pin down.

o o o

If I've sometimes wondered what to do with all the stuff I've accumulated since my dad died, then I've wondered what to do with other things, too. My knowledge, partial though it is, of moments when he erred. My uneasy feelings about the work he did, and its impacts on the world. The end of my parents' marriage. His relationships with my older siblings, who were related to him only by that marriage. Just as I've learnt, in the decades since I first watched the Bush Tucker Man on TV, that there are good reasons to question the cultural archetype of the bushman that I had uncritically idealised as a child—in all of the emotional repression and exclusionary narrowness and potential and actual violence it implies—so I now know that my dad and I would have disagreed, perhaps very strongly, on all kinds of things had he lived longer.

I've struggled, too, to elucidate what I've been doing with my dad's stuff; to find the right metaphor to express my relationship with these objects even as I find myself inexorably drawn to them. Am I a puzzle solver, or an archaeologist attempting to understand the past through the traces its inhabitants have left? A collector aiming to amass a complete set, or something else entirely? Each of these analogies captures some essential element of my relationship with these possessions—my greed for them and the comfort they have brought me; the ways I have used them to fill in the blanks in my knowledge of his life as I have attempted to understand him better. But each expresses only part of the picture while rendering others murky.

The problem with the painting of the bushman is not only that it's ugly, or mysterious, or that it references a culturally weighted and frequently problematic archetype, although each of these things is true. It's that this object could never hope to represent the person my dad was, even as its presence on my wall endeavours to convince me otherwise. Indeed, it has sometimes seemed as though each of the objects I've amassed since my dad died has possessed a mind of its own, vying with the others for primacy. The painting has demanded I remember my dad in one way, but the photograph of him in cap and graduation gown that faces it from across the room has requested, a little more politely, that I recall him in another. Meanwhile, the formal family portrait displayed beside that has had other ideas and hasn't been afraid to let me know, just as that photo of him as a little boy has also made its case. Each has obscured and revealed in turn. Each has allowed me to see him only through the imperfect lens of a piece of smoked glass.

The difficulty of these things is that they are each partly right and partly wrong. Dad was all of these people, but none of them alone: not only a bushman, or a family man, or a scientist, or a kid from a dried-up little town. He was also a person who loved abstract art, and jazz music, and nice wine; who read the kinds of detective novels they sell at airport newsstands, and spoke French fluently, and taught himself to play tennis left-handed when his right elbow gave out. He liked gadgets, and ginger cats, and the soundtrack to the 1983 film *Local Hero*. He drove a ute, but for a while he also had an unreliable old car that was always breaking down. He endured panic attacks, and maintained an unforgiving schedule of work and travel even after he'd been diagnosed with severe depression, but he also had a silly song for every occasion, and never failed to pass a cemetery without cracking a joke about 'the dead centre of town'. He could be short-tempered and arrogant, but he was also funny, and very smart, and unfailingly forthright in his belief in my abilities. Once, when I received a prize at an end-of-year school assembly, he stood and shouted a triumphant 'YES!', much to the consternation of the hushed crowd.

None of my objects capture all of this. And, though they might insist otherwise, none of them ever could.

o o o

I am embarrassed to admit this, but it only occurred to me relatively recently to take the painting off the wall and turn it over, to see if there might be some clue to its origins on the back. That's how I found out that the bushman was from Ireland, not Australia. That's how I found out he wasn't a bushman at all.

The reverse of the painting was bare except for a small slip, tucked up under the tape that bound the frame to the backing board. It told me that the picture had been framed by a company in Shannon, County Clare, Ireland. Armed with this new information, I googled the name signed in the bottom left-hand corner again and found the artist Edward Sylvester Hynes. Born in County Clare in 1897, the seventh of eight children, and raised in Nottingham, he joined the merchant navy and studied medicine before becoming a cartoonist and caricaturist. After retiring to his birthplace, he produced oil paintings and charcoal sketches. He died in 1982.

The pieces all fit, but I wasn't totally convinced until I found a picture of one of Hynes' other paintings online. Titled *The Travelling Horse Dealer*, it might have been the bushman, but for a few details: red hair in place of brown; a cigarette instead of a pipe; a bridle, rather than a beer, in one hand. He had the same crooked nose and bushy brows, the same prominent ears and Adam's apple, the same wonky smile, the same blue eyes. They looked almost as much alike as my dad and the Bush Tucker Man once had.

It turned out that I'd never asked the right questions, not only of the painting but of the other people who'd known my dad. When I did, I found myself hearing stories about an Irish girlfriend and a failed attempt at living in Dublin. It wasn't so much that it mattered if I'd never even known that he'd been to Ireland—not a shocking revelation in itself—and more that the whole episode suggested he had retained his capacity to surprise me.

It reminded me of a sensation that had become familiar in the immediate aftermath of Dad's death, when I'd been haunted by the feeling that his absence wasn't permanent. That I'd answer my phone late one afternoon and hear his voice on the line. It hadn't been that I'd actually expected him to call, of course, but that I'd sensed how, even in death, my dad—or my idea of him—could still change. It occurred to me that this was what I'd treasured about these objects all along: the sense that our relationship had the capacity to continue, in some way, even after he was gone.

Baby Teeth

I hadn't been looking for the baby teeth. Instead, as the summer had given way imperceptibly to autumn, I had succumbed to the decluttering impulse that had been building like late-season humidity.

I'd done the shed first, which had yielded an old esky, a plastic paddling pool, a barely used fishing net and a cobwebby deckchair to be given away on Facebook. I'd cast off the three increasingly rusty bikes that had been parked on the verandah; found a taker for the iPod Nano that worked only when it was connected to a power point.

I'd excavated unworn and unwanted pairs of shoes from the wardrobe, and old pillowcases from the laundry cupboard. Cleaned out the bathroom cabinet, and the kitchen drawers. Thinned out the straggly clusters of pot plants in the back garden, even.

Then I got to the attic, and everything came to a halt. I found a baby-pink velvet jewellery box, about the right size for a necklace. It rattled when shaken gently. Inside, sandwiched in tufts of cottonwool and a sprinkling of faded glitter, were nine of my baby teeth.

When I opened the box and saw them, my initial reaction was repulsion. Then the urge to pick them up and see how they felt in my fingers; to run my thumb over the unexpected sharpness of their undersides and the places where a few had split right down their middles, their exposed insides chalky and brittle.

When I held them in my hand, I felt something like the moment when you realise you're going to cry, but without the unpleasantness that implies. It was a warmth, a fullness. Like missing someone even while you're with them; something expansive, yet contained.

o o o

It took a while to work out what their colour reminded me of, where I had seen that particular shade of brittle off-white. Then my mind turned up an image of the limestone paths that ran through the large bushland reserve on the street where my family lived when I was a child.

It had, in truth, been a long time since I'd thought much about that street. We'd lived there from the time I was an infant until I was on the cusp of my teens, along a stretch of steeply sloping bitumen in Perth's northern suburbs. Homes had lined up along one side of the street, overlooking the bushland on the other and the ocean beyond.

The area had been suburbia since at least the 1970s, but living where we did, it never really felt like that. It wasn't just the storms, which would rattle the windows in their frames as the wind screamed through the narrow gaps around the glass, nor the vivid sweep of the ocean, which would turn steely under a rain-cloud sky.

It was also that reserve, a remnant—a reminder—of the scrub that had once covered the coastal plain. A sea of dense, grey-green foliage threaded through with those whitish walking tracks, their surface blindingly bright in the harsh noontime sun.

Once I started thinking about the bushland reserve, I found that memories of that place and time continued to arrive, inexorable as the tide. I remembered how, at night, when we drove up that street, the verge would be alive with the eyes of feral rabbits, greenish as they reflected in the car headlights. How we'd had a cat that used to kill the rabbits, and how eventually we'd found her, laid out stiff in our backyard, bitten—presumably—by a venomous snake.

How one afternoon, a big dugite had crossed the road and tried to slither up the long window beside our front door, its pale belly pressed against the glass. How our neighbour, an elderly gent who wore white socks with leather sandals year-round, had killed it with a rake. How he'd hung its body over the fence like a warning.

I remembered some of the stories that used to circulate about the bushland. About rumours of a man who made a sport of ambushing women walking on the trails, exposing himself before fleeing into the dunes. About the armed fugitive whose presence had, one particular afternoon, locked down my school while the police searched the brush.

I remembered, too, how my older brother and I used to find things in there—broken prams and discarded beer bottles, rusty chairs and odd shoes. Dumped rubbish, or perhaps the detritus of other people who were drawn to that place.

Later, after my brother had moved out of home, I found a pair of binoculars in a black leather case, stashed beneath the waxy foliage of an acacia near the summit of the dune directly opposite our house. I never told anyone about them, but would retrieve and peer through them each time I visited, scanning the bushland and the coastline through their sights.

That went on for months. Then, one day, I found they'd vanished.

o o o

As a kid, I'd always wanted an attic. Maybe that seems an odd longing for a child to possess, but that's the kind I was prone to being: romantic, a touch dreamy, my imagination fuelled by the Victorian novels my mother had made a regular feature at bedtime, before I gained the ability to read them myself.

In these books, the attic was often the id space, a zone where whatever is transgressive and disruptive could be contained, at least for a time. They were the place where Mr Rochester's 'mad' wife was hidden and where Dorian Gray secreted his hideous painterly avatar. Where, in *Villette*, Lucy is locked alongside 'many black-beetles', 'a very dark and large rat' and the ghost of a nun said to have been buried alive during the Middle Ages.

And yet the kind of attic I have in adulthood—the one where I found my baby teeth—isn't much like any of these. It isn't romantic or spooky or even especially atmospheric. It is dimly lit and oddly shaped, boxed in within a larger roof cavity and constructed from supposedly rodent-proof material that looks a lot like opaque bubble wrap. If you look closely, the whole structure gives the impression of being held together by staples and peeling duct tape.

The poet and critic Susan Stewart has described attics as spaces— like junk drawers—'whose purpose is to hold and preserve things that have lost their functions, even as they have somehow retained enough worth to continue to exist'. Things that are 'beyond surplus'; 'a surplus of surplus'. And so I found the difficulty, when I finally got around to clearing out mine, wasn't just that there was a lot of stuff up there—so much that it was difficult to move around—but also that it had inadvertently become a dumping ground for all the things that I would come to think of as tricky, or stubborn. These items tended to be mementoes: objects that seem to derive their meaning primarily from the stories attached to them, which aren't usually considered necessary but give the impression that they might continue to meet some need nonetheless.

o o o

The colour of the teeth also reminded me of the abalone shells I used to collect from the beach near our house when I was a kid. Their smooth undersides had the same kind of creamy undertone, except on the shells it was overlaid with a silky, pearlescent sheen that reflected light in oily pastel shades of pink and blue and green.

As a child, I was interested in these shells only as a thing of beauty, to be scavenged amid the snarled seaweed beached after storms. But I was aware they were coveted by others; that people from all across our city would flock to the beaches near our home to gather the molluscs that lived inside them within the extremely brief periods and strict bag limits allowed by the local authorities. We would see people out there, on those scant morning hours declared in season, picking their way over the exposed reef at low tide, prising abalone off the rocks and collecting them in mesh bags. I knew that many of the fishers were immigrants from China and their descendants; that abalone was prized in Chinese culture. I also knew, even then, that accidents were not uncommon and that a shocking number of people had drowned while taking part, such were the perils of this stretch of coast and its reefs and unpredictable waves and currents.

Such dangers seemed to be encapsulated by a notorious spot called the Blue Hole, a gap in the reef nestled behind a limestone outcrop, pitted with caves, that was a local landmark. From a distance, even from the shore—where signs warned in the strongest possible terms against swimming in the vicinity—the Blue Hole tended to appear innocuous, depending on the weather. And yet I'd grown up hearing about how nuns had drowned there, as had a racehorse; more than one. How it had been filled in with old cars, or blown up, or both. The stories suggested that if you weren't careful—if you ventured too close—you could be sucked right under and trapped beneath the reef. For my part, I imagined it as a whirlpool, inescapable and unpredictable. But I never dared get close enough to check.

Indeed, despite the many real and varied perils that lurked in those liminal zones between suburbia and open ocean, the Blue Hole was the only one that truly frightened me as a kid. Perhaps I thought, however mistakenly, that I'd be able to avoid the other dangers: I was a strong swimmer, knew to stamp my feet when walking in the bush to alert snakes to my presence, had learnt some basic self-defence manoeuvres during a brief spell of attending martial arts classes at my worried mother's behest. But there was something about the Blue Hole that seemed so inevitable, so subsuming. I couldn't see how you'd get away from it, should it decide to swallow you whole.

o o o

After I found the little pink box, I began to wonder what people usually do with baby teeth—their own, and their children's. A friend told me she'd saved the first tooth her son had lost and buried it in the dirt of a houseplant to keep it close. Another friend, expecting her first child, thought it creepy to save teeth in this way, and couldn't understand why I wouldn't just throw mine in the bin.

When I searched online, I found some parents furtively squirrelled away their kids' milk teeth in an envelope or a drawer, while others proudly retained them in a specially designed wooden box with a slot for each one. Still others discussed having them cryopreserved—'for stem cells'—or even incorporated into a necklace or ring. I wondered what I might do, in their place.

I read, too, that the Victorians were also fond of using baby teeth in jewellery. They weren't the first to do so, but Queen Victoria had set a trend among her contemporaries with pieces including a brooch and a pendant-and-earrings set inlaid with her children's teeth. She also had jewellery that incorporated hair, including at least eight pieces made using strands belonging to her beloved husband, Prince Albert, after his death. Deborah Lutz, a scholar of Victorian literature, has described all of this as part of a resurgence in relic culture—and particularly secular relics—in nineteenth-century Britain, when such objects became sources of comfort for the bereaved, allowing them to keep their lost loved one close.

Baby teeth, of course, are something a little different. In hanging on to them—in having them set like precious stones or hoarding them like jewels—we might remember someone who is no longer with us in a less literal sense. Most of the time, the child in question lives on as an older child or an adolescent or, in my case, an adult. Still, it's possible to detect some sense of loss here, of something meaningful that cannot be recaptured.

o o o

Another thing I liked, as a kid, about those Victorian novels was their heightened emotional tenor. Their romance and melodrama seemed in sympathy with the contours of my own inner life, in which a child's usual inability to reliably regulate emotions was coupled with a tendency to feel things with such intensity that I would not-infrequently become so upset over inconsequential matters that I'd make myself physically sick. (I recall once being sent to the school nurse after being reduced to a sobbing mass after owning up to accidentally causing very minor damage to a key prop for our class nativity play.)

Learning how to deal with such feelings is a normal part of growing up, and there are of course more and less healthy ways of doing so. I remember, very distinctly, schooling myself to tuck my feelings away beneath a calm exterior—to keep my face impassive, and to say nothing rather than risk someone hearing my voice wobble—having gained the strong sense that I would fit in better this way. (I still recall the look of bewilderment on my teacher's face following my tearful confession regarding the manger; the palpable sense that all of this was *far too much* on my part, maybe even a little bit weird and frightening.)

You can see the appeal that books such as *Wuthering Heights* or *Jane Eyre*—with all of their emotional extremes but also their interest in hauntings and things kept hidden and out of sight—might have held for a young person who felt this way. I remember being quite terrified, for example, of Bertha Mason, Charlotte Bronte's so-called 'madwoman' in the attic: seen from the position of Jane's first-person narration, she is hideous and alarming; a destructive, pyromaniac apparition, all demonic laughter and red eyes and far-off murmurs.

But I was also undeniably compelled by her fearsome outbursts and powerful, creeping presence.

Years later, at university, I wrote my Honours dissertation on Bertha and came to recognise the ways her 'madness' is not only gendered but also racialised (she is depicted as a Creole woman whose family is said to have concealed their history of 'idiots and maniacs through three generations' prior to her marriage to Rochester). I also learnt about how such a diagnosis was used to exert control over women deemed 'unruly' or in some way disruptive or disobedient according to the social standards of nineteenth-century Britain, and the way Jean Rhys later responded to all of this by sympathetically reimagining Bertha as a young woman named Antoinette in her classic postcolonial novel, *Wide Sargasso Sea*.

I was ignorant of this context during my earlier readings—just as, when I was wandering in the dunes near my house as a kid I was oblivious to being on land stolen from the Whadjuk Noongar people during the same era that Bronte was writing and Queen Victoria was (not coincidentally) overseeing her expanding empire and having her children's teeth set in gilt. But I must have clocked, at some level, the price Bertha pays for her transgressive qualities, among them her lack of emotional restraint. (Spoiler alert, if one is necessary for a novel that's more than 175 years old: she is depicted as comprehensively dehumanised and animalistic in her utterances and behaviour, and eventually dies in a fire lit by her own hand, leaping from the roof of Rochester's manor and thus freeing him to marry the spirited but resolutely self-controlled Jane.)

Either way, by the time I reached puberty—with all the hormonal turbulence that time typically entails—I was well on my way to maintaining an emotional life that was, in many ways, split. My feelings seemed to fluctuate between existing mostly in a deeply private place out of sight of most others, and occasionally making themselves known via up-swellings of hiccupping, snot-soaked tears that would invariably surprise me and those around me with their intensity.

To a significant extent, this was normal adolescent stuff. But it did develop into a problem, perhaps at the point it became apparent this tendency had well and truly outlasted the usual span of teenage tumult. I remember realising this while working in an early journalism job, when a colleague good-naturedly told me I'd make someone a wonderful wife one day because I was so calm all the time. As a statement, it was a rich text in all sorts of weird and dubious ways, but one that struck me at the time mainly because my apparent placidity seemed so at odds with the way I tended to feel inside. It was the same kind of feeling as when a chaperone on a school camp had described me as a 'strong, silent type': an odd way to describe a twelve-year-old girl, but also a reflection of the mismatch between my inner life and the unruffled exterior I was trying very hard to present in public.

I wouldn't have realised it back then, but this tension between self-restraint and release also made itself felt when, a few years later, I began to experience panic attacks. They continue to manifest in the same way today: an escalating dread and a floating sensation that quickly climbs like a cresting wave only to break into an intense, all-encompassing bodily fear characterised by the brief certainty that I, and probably everyone I have ever cared about, will imminently face overwhelming and inescapable catastrophe. This predictability is in many ways a blessing: after I learnt to identify what was happening, these incidents lost a lot of their power to distress. But the fact that they always occurred when I was in bed, drifting towards sleep, seemed telling. I came to think of them almost like a riptide whose inexorable undertow I could resist most of the time, but which might pull me under when my defences were low or the water level high.

o o o

For a long time, I avoided going back to that dune, that bushland, that beach where I grew up. I had no reason to visit: my mother had moved to the country; my school friends and I closer to the city. Moreover, I was at an age where sprawling suburbs can come to seem confining and—worse—dull. After a while, not visiting became more a habit than a conscious choice. Then, one afternoon, I got in the car and made the trip to our old street, surprised to find how little time it took.

The familiar sweep of houses along one side of the road had been rendered gappy by redevelopment, but the limestone paths were still painfully bright in the afternoon sun, and the rustling in the bushes made me flinch. The scrub rewarded a lingering gaze, revealing its subtleties amid the multitudinous green: the red bristles of a one-sided bottlebrush in bloom; the feathery swathes of speargrass seed heads; the small, silvery leaves of the saltbush. The differing foliage of the various plants each produced distinctive noises in the late afternoon breeze: the murmur of the acacia bushes; the sword-sedges, whose strappy leaves seemed almost to sing.

I was pleased to see that there was still a ribbon of greyish sand branching through the bush to the top of the highest dune. That, when I stood on the summit, the wind still carried a smell off the ocean that felt as familiar as breathing. And yet. Half buried in the sand: a metal bottle cap, the remains of a plastic-bottle bong. The rumble of a nearby main road. Less wildness than I'd remembered. The water around where I knew the Blue Hole to be looked calm, even inviting, under the clear, cloudless sky.

o o o

Following my visit to the reserve, I found myself wondering about those binoculars I found in the dunes when I was a kid. About who they might have belonged to and why they'd left them and the direction in which they might've been pointed.

I've thought about all the things you can see from the top of those dunes. About bird watchers, and ship spotters, even whale watchers. But my mind has always come back to our old house, and those of our former neighbours, lined up across the street, their curtains open wide as eyes. Of the dark windows facing not only the dunes and those blinding-white paths and whatever else the bushland might have harboured, but also the ocean and the far-off horizon.

I've thought, too, about why I've felt drawn to the street that fronts onto the bushland but not to the road where we lived immediately afterwards, a more resolutely suburban thoroughfare a few minutes' drive further inland. The reasons didn't seem difficult to parse. When we lived in that first house, my parents were still seemingly happily married and my dad still alive. When we lived there, I hadn't yet been told by a psychologist that getting to the bottom of why I could so often seem so calm even as anxiety fizzed beneath my skin would be crucial to helping it to abate; hadn't yet sat in a chair across from another psychologist and asked her how I could stop these emotional outpourings from bursting forth at the most inopportune times. (Hadn't been told, albeit in gentler words, that I was basically missing the point.)

But I think that view might be in part a trick of distance, even a kind of nostalgia. Though I am tempted to view the years we lived there as some sort of idealised time, it's easy to forget that I was not only an essentially contented and well-cared for child—one surrounded with care and affection—but also a sensitive and deeply fretful one who often felt most comfortable alone. That I hadn't only feared the Blue Hole, back then, but also having to interact with strangers and the unseen threats I was certain lurked in the dark, as well as the guy with the coat full of bees I'd seen in a movie I'd watched at a sleepover, and answering the phone, and the significance of the russet-red stain I'd found in the gusset of my underwear one morning.

Indeed, by the time we moved away from that street, I was already a couple of years into puberty, on the brink of starting high school but still some way from beginning to understand how, as Melissa Febos observes in her book *Girlhood*, 'that what was happening to my body changed my value in the world' in ways that were often uncomfortable and confusing. I'd had my first boyfriend; had been dumped by him the day after Valentine's (he just couldn't imagine marrying his first girlfriend, he'd said). Not so long after that, my parents told me that my dad would be moving out. It was the first time I remember learning this painful lesson: that being a strong swimmer or learning self-defence could not always prevent bad things from happening.

I recall, of course, how upset I was at this news, but also how quickly I managed to pull myself together afterwards. When a friend came around for a pre-arranged visit a few hours later, my memory suggests I managed to appear almost unconcerned when I told her what had happened.

o o o

While I was writing this essay, I revisited *Villette*, and realised that there was more to its attic than I had remembered. That, although Lucy was disgusted by its insects and rodents, and frightened at the prospect of its haunting, she also found in it a freedom from the surveillance she was subjected to elsewhere in the house. That later, when she received a letter from the object of her unrequited affections, she took it up to the attic to read undisturbed.

This solitude was ultimately short-lived: Lucy was surprised by the spectral nun, later revealed to be a friend's suitor. But re-reading this scene, I found other memories from other beloved books, from childhood and beyond, began to emerge. The March sisters staging meetings of their secret society in the garret, and Jo retreating to the place she considers her 'refuge' to write her novel. Maggie's 'favourite retreat on a wet day' in *The Mill on the Floss*, where she might fret 'out all her ill humours' with the—admittedly alarming—assistance of a much-abused fetish doll. Even the narrator in 'The Yellow Wallpaper' who, deprived of writing materials, attempts to exercise her creative impulses on the walls of her fortified room at the top of the house, finding within its patterns figures that mirror her own imprisonment.

Here, then, was another way to imagine the attic and the objects contained within it: not just as a threatening space, but also as a generative one. A place where things might be tumbled together, and take on new significances as a result; where you might keep safe something you're unsure how to handle until you're better equipped to understand.

∘ ∘ ∘

We did manage to clean up our attic eventually, although the credit does not lie with me. I spent weeks dithering and tinkering, discarding a couple of old magazines here and a stack of CDs there. Eventually, I let my partner, David, take over. Somehow, he managed to arrange everything in a way that made the space navigable without having to throw much away.

A little jewellery box filled with baby teeth was never going to make much of a difference in all of this. But I went back and forth about what to do with them. For a while, I was taken with the idea of bringing the box to the bushland and flinging its contents into the scrub: it seemed a way to bring things full circle, almost like scattering a loved one's ashes.

And yet something always held me back, that same thing which had made me hold on to them for so long. It was a warmth, a fullness, a feeling. A sense that I might want to continue to feel their sharp edges in my palm.

The Things We Live With, Part I

'Perhaps all anxiety might derive from a fixation on moments—an inability to accept life as ongoing.' (Sarah Manguso)

o o o

Around 10.30 or 11, the time I usually take my first break from work for the day. The routine rarely changes. Fill the kettle, turn it on, see the orange light glow. Retrieve the cup, shut the rattling drawer, fill the strainer with tea in a puff of dust smelling of cinnamon and star anise. All of this, as unconscious as breathing. Then four steps to the fridge, to open the door and fetch the milk.

But the other morning, as I pulled the handle, one of the magnets fastened to the front leapt to the floor. It was one of the dozens I'd acquired during the years I worked as a travel writer: a cowboy boot, the word 'Texas' printed on its side. The magnet affixed to the back snapped off as it clattered against the jarrah boards. I picked up the pieces. I could mend it. I might need to buy some superglue.

I'd almost forgotten I owned this object, yet my eyes must have passed over it and all the others almost every day I was at home. So I stood there, stuck in place, trying to remember when and where exactly in Texas I'd bought it. It might have been the day we went to the college football game in Austin, or the night we watched a country band at a dance hall. It might have been the day we ordered heaped plates of enchiladas at a restaurant near the turnoff for a town called Eldorado, or the day we tried on cowboy hats in a shop that also sold rhinestone-encrusted belts and pink-satin moccasins. It might even have been the afternoon we drove through far-west Texas, from Marfa to Fort Davis, going nowhere in a hurry.

It's funny, the way we stop seeing the things we live with. Until, that is, they fall from the fridge and break.

o o o

It's customary, when you're telling a story about being unwell, to begin with your worst moment. The moment you cracked, broke down, hit rock bottom—whatever you're supposed to say. But I cannot pinpoint such a moment, when my mind crossed some notional threshold between whole and damaged, healthy and injured, well and ill. Instead, the process was something more gradual, in which—like the apocryphal boiled frog—I mostly failed to notice the changes.

Still, every story needs a place to start. So I'll start on that afternoon in far-west Texas; the afternoon it became apparent I could no longer ignore the shifts that had been taking place.

We were driving through the high desert, the landscape tinted green through the hire car's windows. The yellow grass seemed a sickly hue; the red rocks washed out and grey. Anxieties both mundane and specific had been piling up over the preceding months. I'd been lonely, and stressed at work, and sleeping poorly. David had been away on tour, and each night I would check the doors and windows and windows and doors and then set the alarm and check that a few times, too. Many of my friends were getting married and having babies, and though I wanted neither for the time being, I feared missing out. I was falling out of love with a job I'd once adored, and yet quite often the office was the only place where things made sense. I was always tired, but always on edge; dissatisfied, but unable to make a change. My brain felt blank, though my thoughts raced. I was stuck, I suppose.

A psychologist I later saw told me that this state of being has a name—generalised anxiety disorder, combined with major depressive disorder—but back then I thought of it as an emotional tinnitus, a nonstop dissonant hum that can wear you down to your bones. It was almost sticky, an ever-present pull beneath my belly button and at the back of my throat, like the tension when you hold two magnets, close together but not touching: that sense of waiting for a moment of resolve, of relief, that in this case never comes.

I was a fretful kid who'd become an anxious adult, so I'd had periods like this before. They usually passed after a day or week or month or two, and I'd been sure a holiday would put things right. But we'd been away for one week, then two, and I wasn't feeling better. I'd had a panic attack the night before in the very cool but not especially com-fortable vintage Airstream in which we were staying. But that wasn't the worst of it. The worst of it was the realisation that made itself known as David and I broached the subject of how terrible I'd been feeling and the things I might do about it: that whatever this was, it wasn't going away on its own.

o o o

I can remember the first fridge magnet I bought after I became a travel writer, and started travelling a lot for work. I was on a trip through Portugal and Spain with two dozen other travel writers, and I'd fallen into an easy companionship with a pair of fellow Australians. One was an older guy, funny, who was a keen fridge magnet collector. He teased me when I told him that David wasn't eager to display any magnets on the front of the fridge. I said that David thought they were tacky and cheap-looking, and rightly received the response that the tackiness, the cheapness, was precisely the point. Perhaps because of that, I brought home the most outrageous example I could find: a pair of flamenco dancers with orange skin, the woman's skirt rendered three-dimensional by layers of stiffly ruffled polyester. It was funny and silly and ridiculous, but it didn't take long for the image on the front to start to peel away from its backing.

I've wondered, maybe more than might seem normal, about what I was hoping to achieve in acquiring all the fridge magnets currently displayed in my kitchen. There have certainly been times when I've grown irritated with myself for the acquisitive urge their presence seems to suggest—just as, when I was working as a travel writer, I felt increasingly discomfited to be flying all around the world, playing a role in inflating an acute climate crisis and in promoting an industry (tourism) whose impacts on the world I was not necessarily convinced balanced out for the better. And yet it also seemed to me that there was something going on beyond rampant consumerist covetousness with these objects—or something that existed in addition to it, at least.

Indeed, researchers who study souvenirs have various theories about why we collect them: as markers of status, for the pleasure of spending, simply because we're expected to buy things when we play the role of tourist. There's something in all these ideas, but more compelling to me is the notion that, in buying these objects, we're trying to hang on to being away, to insert some remnant of how it felt into our everyday lives. Design scholar Beverly Gordon has written about the 'concretising function' of souvenirs, the way their 'physical presence helps locate, define, and freeze in time a fleeting, transitory experience, and bring back into ordinary experience something of the quality of an extraordinary experience'. Undergirding this is the assumption that being away and at home are fundamentally different; that the former exists quite outside of and in opposition to the mundane reality of the latter. And, of course, the even greater assumption: that it's possible to freeze a moment in time.

When I was buying my fridge magnets, I suppose I'd hoped they might punctuate a routine trip to the fridge with fond memories; a splash of travel nostalgia stirred into a workday cup of tea. That retrieving my morning yoghurt might recall an afternoon cycling in the sunshine through a small Dutch city, thanks to a dinky pair of wooden clogs.

That fetching leftovers for lunch might remind me of ordering at a hawker centre in Singapore, by way of a miniaturised rendition of a bowl of noodles. That seeing these magnets would remind me of being away; of forgetting myself, for a second.

But if 'home' and 'away' are separate states, then there must, by definition, be some border between our experience of them. Such a boundary is impossible to locate. Did I cease feeling at home when I stepped into the Uber outside our house, or when I checked in at the airport? When I boarded the plane and settled into my allotted seat? When did that feeling of 'away' set in, and why was I so ill-at-ease even in the places that were supposed to feel most like home? What, too, of the boundary between anxious and not; where does that fall? I hadn't yet realised how arbitrary and porous the line between 'well' and 'ill' can be; the way I might seem to slide back and forth across it within the space of hours or even minutes, depending not only on how I felt at any moment but also the circumstances that surrounded me. Hadn't yet realised how often this can be the case with mood disorders like mine: the way their symptoms are quite often amplified versions of 'normal' feelings and sensations rendered clinically and person- ally significant by intensity and longevity and a resultant power to cause distress.

The fridge magnets similarly make a lie of such binaries. They are both domestic and foreign, useful and not. Like memories, they change with time; grow dusty and their colours dull. In becoming a part of our homes, they also become part of our ordinary lives; begin to lose their veneer of 'away'. They grow familiar, as our eyes slip over them, like a river over rocks.

o o o

When I first got a job as a travel writer, I stuck a quote by the travel writer Paul Theroux on the wall in front of my desk. The best writers are scrupulous noticers, it read. My editor at the time liked to say that we were 'trained noticers'. That it was our job to go into the world, and see what it was like, and report back.

I found that I could practise this skill. That I could go for a walk and resolve to notice everything I passed that was red, or yellow, or blue. That I could sit and make lists of everything I could see. The point was to allow my focus to puddle and grow deep. To become sodden with detail, with that crystalline stillness of stopping, for a second.

I became good at noticing certain things. The items on sale at a street market in a mid-sized Chinese city. The patter of a Boston tour guide. The small creatures that scuttled into the sand as I picked my way through the mangroves in Roebuck Bay at low tide. I told myself that noticing these things was a kind of mindfulness, a way of standing still in a life that sometimes felt relentlessly peripatetic.

I liked the feeling this gave me, that sense of being purposeful and engaged and busy. It wasn't that my anxiety disappeared when I was away, but that I tended to be so caught up in what was going on around me that I noticed it less. By dialling up the unfamiliarity of my surroundings, I could turn down—or tune out—the background noise of my brain. By noticing the street markets and the tour guides and the small creatures, I could avoid noticing other things, and distract from that ever-unresolved tension, that pull beneath my ribcage, that pressure behind my brows.

And yet, in hindsight, I can see that I wasn't standing still in all those moments but swimming against an undertow while trying to pretend it wasn't so. That all the while, the thing the poet Mark Halliday calls 'the sheer ongoingness of life'—'its involuntary momentum, day, night, day, night, day...'—was continuing to pull me out to sea.

o o o

There's a temptation, in writing this story. To describe how, not long after we got home from Texas, I went to the doctor and cried, and told her what was going on. How she handed me a box of tissues and told me there were lots of things I could try. I'm tempted, too, to list all those things I went on to try: the medications and breathing exercises, the changes to diet and exercise and daily routine, the mindfulness apps and the scratchy fabric of the chairs in psychologists' waiting rooms.

Part of me thinks such a list might be helpful to someone like the person I have been, who wants to know what they, too, might try. Part of me also wants to demonstrate what a 'good' patient I have been: how diligent in my willingness to try anything that might help. And yet another part of me is aware of the ways these kinds of lists by 'good' patients like me might be used to berate those who are judged less 'diligent', less 'conscientious', and thus less 'deserving' of care and concern.

I know how lucky I have been, to have all these things to try. Indeed, though it didn't feel like it at the time, I can now see the spectacular good fortune of many of the moments I have described. That I had a partner who understood something was seriously wrong and encouraged me to seek help. A doctor who knew what to say and how she might assist. That I could get an appointment with her, and with the psychologist she referred me to (no small thing, given the current shortage of the latter in Australia); could afford the gap payments to see them both in private practice. That they both believed and validated my distress, perhaps in part because I am a white, middle-class cis woman, and thus am less likely to have my reports regarding my own wellbeing discounted (there is, for example, considerable research from multiple countries pointing to evidence of gender, racial and other forms of bias in the treatment of pain). That I wasn't dealing with additional layers of disadvantage or discrimination or prejudice on top of a situation that was difficult enough with the resources and advantages available to me.

I was also ashamed. Ashamed of how, at times, an unkind word or an errant look has held the power to knock my whole day askew. How I have ruminated for entire afternoons and evenings over a careless thing that someone has said or done, even when—especially when—that someone was me. How I have felt guilty I could not cope when so many people who deal with far worse have far less support, but also felt guilty for feeling guilty, which helps absolutely no one. How I have worried I am not 'sick enough' to write about my experiences because I have largely been able to maintain the outward markers of societal 'success' throughout my illness. And yet—and I do not want to sound glib here—how sick would qualify as 'enough'?

When I was a travel writer, people often asked me whether I needed someone to carry my suitcases on my next trip; often told me I had the best job in the world. My colleagues and I agreed the only appropriate response was effusive agreement. And so part of me—a large, noisy part—hesitates to describe the work trips I went on when I was anxious and depressed, because no one needs to hear someone who had 'the best job in the world' complaining about it. Instead of describing those trips, I was going to write some more about my fridge magnets, make them work like a metaphor by standing in for the things I didn't want to talk about. There'd be a crocodile, mouth agape, from Broome. A red tram from Lisbon. A bowl of noodles, painstakingly selected during a long wait at the airport in Hong Kong. I was going to do that, and so I went into the kitchen, and removed those three magnets from the fridge so that I could line them up on my desk.

As I stood there, turning them over in my hands, I thought about how I once saw or read or heard someone describe anxiety as a form of stuck-ness. To understand the metaphor, it's necessary to know a little about how the condition works. That the physical symptoms of anxiety are normal biological responses to a perceived threat that causes physiological changes in the body—faster breathing to increase oxygen in the blood; an elevated heartbeat to pump that oxygen into your major muscle groups—intended to help you react. This is often called the fight, flight or freeze response, and when the threat is something like those our ancestors would have faced—a wild animal, say—it is generally helpful and appropriate: it might help us run away from the danger, or fend it off. But it is less helpful and often counterproductive in the face of the threats that I, for example, might habitually encounter today. Especially when—as whoever-it-was suggested was the case for me—this response gets stuck in the 'on' position, like a faulty lever or a car jammed in the wrong gear.

This reminds me of the final trip I went on before I stopped working as a travel writer: not a work trip but a family holiday, to Bali. It was January, sticky and humid, and every time I stepped outside the air-conditioning my glasses fogged against my face. My brain felt somehow similar.

I tried to focus my mind on the present moment by noticing details in the way I'd trained myself. I took photos on my phone of frangipani flowers against grey pavements, and loose-limbed dogs sprawled under plastic awnings. Of snails ascending a wooden post, and a baby-blue truck piled high with pineapples. Of spun-sugar clouds, and a young woman posing on the beach against a bruised sky. But I found the old trick was no longer working. I'd no sooner notice a detail than it would slip away like a wave, and I'd be left with that tension, those magnets, hovering half-an-inch apart.

o o o

When I was a travel writer, I tried to notice the things I was seeing so I could write about them afterwards. But it was, as Mark Halliday has written, like 'paddling in the river while you try to see the river as a whole'. It was impossible to notice all of it, to capture everything in my notebook or my camera or even my mind. It was inevitable that I should forget or miss something, despite my best efforts to the contrary.

In her book *Ongoingness*, Sarah Manguso writes in this way about her decades-long practice of keeping a daily diary. 'I didn't want to lose anything,' she says; and by 'anything', she means the moments that accumulate to form a life. Her diary was a way to 'avoid getting lost in time'; a defence against 'waking up at the end of my life and realizing I'd missed it'. 'I wrote so I could truly say I was paying attention,' she says. I've wondered if this is what I was trying to do with my fridge magnets.

We tend to talk about fridge magnets in a similar way to my travelling companion from that work trip to Spain: as kitsch, silly, meaningless; the tackier the better. But when you think about it, the thing they do—the thing we do with them—is much more complex, more interesting, than that. They allow us to feel that, in bartering for them and buying them and bringing them back and displaying them in our homes, we're hanging on to a moment—concretising the extraordinary, attempting to distil its essence into a physical thing that seems less vulnerable to change than the mutable, unreliable medium that is memory. Indeed, as I removed the crocodile from my fridge, I thought of coming in to land at Broome airport, the landscape below reduced to patterns of colour and texture. I held the red tram in my palm and thought of custard tarts with a yolk-bright filling and yellow buildings under a low, grey sky. I removed the bowl of noodles with a gentle tug and, as the magnet gave way, remembered elderly men with songbirds in wooden cages and neon lights in Kowloon at dusk. These things might only be clumsy pieces of colourful plastic designed with reference to crude stereotypes, but they seemed to encapsulate moments, memories—even whole cities and towns—in their form.

The truth, of course, is more complicated. Though we might imagine we can freeze a picture of a place in our recollections and store it in a piece of tourist tat, neither places nor memory really work that way. Just as memories are remade each time we recall them, the communities where people live are constantly changing. Both Hong Kong and Texas have changed, in some important and disturbing ways, since I last visited. Everywhere is at least a little altered due to the turmoil of the last few years, and not necessarily for the better. This is one reason a magnet makes a partial and imperfect stand-in for moments and scenes and stories.

Another is that the things these magnets recall are not always the ones they might have brought forth the day before, or the day after; aren't always the ones I want them to recollect. The crocodile also reminds me how lonely I often was in strange hotel rooms. Of the night when I was unable to sleep because I felt jumpy and paranoid, fearing a too-friendly resort security guard might have followed me back to my room in the dark. Of the many nights when I'd checked those doors and windows and maybe even under the hotel-room bed. Of the days I felt I was getting dumped by breakers I should have been surfing instead. This is part of the reason writing about all of this feels tricky: if I write about those times, then I'm not writing about the other ones. If I write about the stuff that felt bad, then I'm not writing about the good, or the in-between (where does *that* border lie?). Just as the souvenir appears to simplify the complexity of a place into a piece of plastic, so too can recounting an experience seem to diminish it, fail to capture all of its various and often conflicting parts.

This is one of the difficulties of writing about those magnets that reside in my chest and my guts and my brow. My experience of mental illness has been of something that has refused to be pinned down by catch-all words such as 'anxiety'—which we ask, after all, to describe not only a whole range of serious health conditions but also our nerves before a big presentation at work, excited jitters before a holiday, a certain keenness ('I am anxious to do my best'), and a source of concern ('that's a real anxiety for me'). It has, for me, been the experience of two or more seemingly conflicting things sometimes being true at the same time: of being lucky and not; unwell and yet largely able to function. Indeed, if my anxiety is like a car over-revving while stuck in the wrong gear, then for me depression is what ensues when such a state becomes too acute, too prolonged; when the engine overheats or the car veers into a mire and becomes stuck in a somewhat different way. Having both has thus often been an experience of paradoxical things being true simultaneously: of feeling as though I'm wading through mud, but also being unable to settle; of my thoughts racing even as my mind feels fuzzy; of being unable to sleep, but also exhausted. Of feeling stuck, but also adrift.

And though an essay allows more room for nuance than a fridge magnet, the problem that writing one presents is similar. Both attempt to transform an experience into something solid that you can hold in your hands or your mind. Into writing, or souvenirs, or memories; something that partially represents, rather than preserves. Each feels like paddling round a bend while trying to see the full stretch of the river.

o o o

At this point in a story about being unwell, it's customary to describe how you got better. How things slowly but surely improved. How, eventually, you were cured. It's difficult to resist these kinds of narrative rhythms—these beats of rock bottom, remedy, recovery—even when you set out intending to do so. They can feel inexorable, like a river draining to an estuary. That this essay reproduces some of these patterns attests, perhaps, to their magnetism. And though I can recognise the hard-won hope they provide to people desperately in need of it, I also want to recognise that, for me—and many others, I think—things have not been quite so linear.

And I did get better, although there were also times when I got worse, and then a bit better, and then much worse. A year or so after I first went to doctor, I had another appointment in which I admitted that suicidal thoughts had begun spilling into my mind, hot flashes of electricity that arrived as sudden and unwelcome as a summer storm on Christmas morning. If I thought I'd cried a lot during my earlier visit, it was nothing compared to that day.

At those times, the options seemed binary: I was ill, but wanted to be well, and the two appeared to exist only in opposition to one another. At those times, my greatest worry was that I had 'broken my brain'—that was the phrase I always used—in some irreversible way. I said this to a psychologist once, and she suggested that I might focus instead on feeling just a little better, and then a little better than that. It seemed like a place from which I could start.

In the years since, I have mostly gotten better, in that I've had no days or weeks or months as bad as that day was. I have gotten so much better that I've had hours and days and maybe weeks where the anxiety has been reduced to something tolerable. But, in this context, 'better' exists as a relative term rather than an end point, and 'recovery' as an ongoing process—a verb rather than a noun. I am aware my progress is precarious. There have continued to be days and weeks and months when that familiar tension has felt exhausting and all-consuming. More recently, I have begun to let go of the idea of being cured. Instead, I have been trying to find ways to live with this thing that continues to show no consistent signs of going away.

Indeed, I've wondered, while I've been writing this essay, whether it would be better—for the purposes of the story I'm telling—to mend that cowboy-boot magnet or leave it broken in two. I thought mending it might feel like a gesture toward a happy ending, and we all want one of those. But also that leaving it in pieces seemed more realistic.

o o o

Back when I was still a travel writer, someone I used to work with would drive me to distraction with his constant, ebullient ideas and suggestions and new projects. 'At least you get to go home at the end of the day,' he'd tell me. 'I'm stuck with myself.'

Alain de Botton writes about something like this in *The Art of Travel*, in a passage about going to the Caribbean. He recounts waking up early on his first morning and sitting by the sea, describing the view before him, which he 'recognised from the brochure'. And yet he acknowledges this description 'only imperfectly' reflects what is occurring within him. He's also aware of 'a sore throat that I had developed during the flight, a worry at not having informed a colleague that I would be away, a pressure across both temples and a rising need to visit the bathroom'. He realises, with disappointment or horror: 'I had inadvertently brought myself with me to the island.'

Sarah Manguso writes about this, too, in another of her books. 'If you go to Paris, you won't find Paris; you'll find yourself in Paris,' she says.

'You might as well stay home. There, where the surrounding environment fades to neutral, you'll really find yourself, but only if you're really looking.'

It wasn't until quite recently that I realised *Ongoingness* is a kind of recovery narrative; that it documents the way Manguso learnt to let go of her obsessive diary-keeping and the unease it exemplified. The catalyst was the birth of her first child, after which she became absorbed by the demands—simultaneously relentless and monotonous—of his care. She thus began 'to inhabit time differently'. She surrendered to 'the wave of mortality'; the knowledge that 'time will go on without' her. She stopped trying to notice so much, trying to record her life so minutely. She forgot things and realised nothing terrible happened as a result. She came to understand 'that the forgotten moments are the price of continued participation in life'. She no longer struggled against the ongoingness of existence, but allowed its current to carry her downstream.

A Small, Brown Suitcase

1 x collection of old coins

1 x small notebook with an orange plastic cover

2 x watches in need of repair

1 x pouch of documents relating to my grandfather's job

2 x large envelopes of family pictures, mainly in black and white

3 x condolence cards sent to my grandfather after my grandmother's death

1 x packet of photographic negatives

o o o

A simple way to describe the small, brown suitcase would be to say that it contains an assortment of objects that once belonged to my paternal grandfather. Papers, and photographs, and bits and pieces. Some obsolete foreign currency, stored in a cigarette tin. Two broken watches, in a wooden cigar box. (I guess he was a smoker.)

A better way to describe the suitcase would be to say that it contains nearly everything I have ever known about my father's father. That it has long been an object of fascination for me, even before my dad died and every item even tangentially connected to his life took on a new and special significance.

I never met my grandfather, and my dad never talked much about his parents or his childhood beyond the usual clichés about sleeping on the verandah in a flour sack and walking ten miles to school each day. His past, in general, always appeared opaque to me. The main things I remember hearing about his father were scraps of stories about how he'd been disappointed my dad hadn't followed him down the coal mines into a 'job for life'; this idea that my dad had—in spite of his successes—been something of a disappointment. Everything else, more or less, I have gleaned from the artefacts my grandfather left behind in this small, brown suitcase.

One of the most compelling objects contained within it has, for me, always been a little orange notebook, which my grandfather appears to have used as an address book. Within its pages, it's possible to track the passing of time as the lists of addresses and telephone numbers are updated when people move. It includes three addresses for my father: one in Canberra, where he moved from Queensland to do his Honours year at university; one in New York State, where he went to do his PhD; and one in Sydney, where he later lived as a young geologist, newly married to a French woman he'd met in America.

The notebook charts, in much the same way, my grandfather's moves, from the small town in north Queensland where my dad grew up to another coal mining town nearby, then to Brisbane, and then again further south, where his final residence was a nursing home in suburban Sydney. The notebook also includes jottings about doctor's appointments and bus routes, and workings out for sums. As you turn the pages, the handwriting gradually deteriorates. By the end of the notebook, it is almost illegible.

o o o

I have wondered why this orange notebook, among all the other things in the suitcase, stands out for me as it does. Roland Barthes' twinned concepts of the 'studium' and the 'punctum', described in *Camera Lucida*, have helped me to get at the distinction, just as they allowed Barthes to explain why he felt so deeply invested in and affected by some photographic images but not others.

The studium describes an attraction that is more general, more rational, more intellectual, perhaps; something 'of the order of *liking*, not of *loving*' that speaks to a photograph's cultural and historical context. You might say that the studium of the suitcase—of the address book—is all the assorted information, the names and notes that it offers up. These details have always intrigued me; have provided a series of traces to be interpreted; a riddle to be solved.

But the orange notebook—and, specifically, my grandfather's worsening handwriting—affects me in a different way. It is, for me, what Barthes called the punctum: in Latin, a puncture, a wound, but also *a point*. The punctum refers to something more intense and less predictable, which belongs to the realm of emotional and bodily sensation. Barthes characterised it as 'the element which rises from the scene, shoots out of it like an arrow, and pierces me'; 'that accident which pricks me (but also bruises me, is poignant to me)'.

This handwriting inflicts a sting. There is something sharp in the way its neat curlicues become shaky and uneven as I turn the pages, signalling the slow decline of my grandfather's health. How, like the rusty stains denoting the high-water line on a bridge, it suggests the now-absent hand that made these marks. How, when I run a finger across the indentations it has left in the paper, I can imagine the nib of my grandfather's pen scratching at the surface, even if I cannot quite picture how his face might have looked, angled over the page, as it did so.

○ ○ ○

1964–72   10 Abbott Street, Oonoonba

1974–76   3 Fraser Street, Moranbah

1978   41 Ellis Street, Kangaroo Point

1978   9 Pharlap Parade, Mackay

1979   Lowson House, Brisbane Hospital

1979   7 Murray Street, Wilston

1986   Avoca Nursing Home, Randwick

○ ○ ○

I tried, once, to map out my grandfather's life using the address book and some of the other things in the suitcase. I still have the piece of paper showing my workings: a list of addresses and dates gleaned from letters; names, notes, his date of birth.

It is a deeply unsatisfying document, in part because it tells me a lot of bland facts and little else, but also because it makes visible the gaps that the items in the small, brown suitcase leave in the chronology of my grandfather's life. How they have nothing to say about his childhood, or his arrival in Australia from his birthplace in Scotland, or what exactly he might have been doing before he married my grandmother just after the end of the Second World War.

Perhaps another reason this list is unsatisfying is because everything I have ever been able to find out about my grandfather has been overshadowed to the point of near-total eclipse by knowing how his life ended. By knowing that after my grandmother died quite suddenly in her mid-fifties, my grandfather had what used to be known as a nervous breakdown. That later, he underwent electroshock therapy. That he never really recovered.

The reasons for my grandfather's breakdown are still unclear to me, but they were always presented as self-evident in the tale as it was repeated within my family. Perhaps my grandfather had been one of those men of his generation unused to meeting his own basic needs; I was always told, in a way that suggested the information was significant, that my grandmother had even handled the family finances. But there is another possibility that I find piercingly poignant: that perhaps he was lonely without her; that he simply missed her too much.

o o o

It was only quite recently that I realised there was a problem with the story I had heard growing up, about how my dad had been a disappointment to his father. The problem was a letter I found in the suitcase. Addressed 'to whom it may concern', it informs the reader that my grandfather had, as of April 15, 1964, accrued thirty-one years of continuous service at the mine. That he was one of thirty men who had recently been retrenched. 'He has proved reliable and conscientious,' it reads, 'and has always carried out his duties in a satisfactory manner.'

That word—*satisfactory*—seemed to reach out of the page. For me, the word itself was a punctum. To have thirty-one years of work summed up so dismissively.

Also, in the letter, my grandfather's surname is spelled incorrectly.

At the time this letter was written, my grandfather would have been a couple of years shy of his fiftieth birthday and my dad would have been nearly sixteen, studying at the grammar school in a larger town nearby. Perhaps it took my grandfather a little time to realise that finding a new job at a mine would not be straightforward, as some of the papers in the suitcase seem to suggest. Even so, the timing struck me as significant, and made me wonder whether my grandfather's disappointment that my dad hadn't followed him there might have been based in something else entirely.

Sometime after my dad left his hometown to go to grammar school, and then university and then another university and another, it must have become apparent to his parents that he was headed towards a life quite different from their own. That he wouldn't marry a local girl and have local children and become a part of the local community. That he was growing into a person his parents had not necessarily expected him to become.

I had a conversation with my mum not so long ago about my dad, and why he never spoke much about his childhood. And she pointed out that, in becoming the first person in his family to go to university, he was doing more than leaving his hometown or opting for a different job. My grandfather's father had been a coal miner, as had his father, and his father's father, and so on. In failing to follow his father down the mine, my dad had rejected not only a job 'for life' but also, implicitly, a way of life.

It's easy to imagine my grandparents being pleased my dad was getting opportunities that they hadn't—to re-tell the stories about how his mother, bursting with pride after he received his PhD, insisted on always referring to him as Dr Nisbet. It is less comfortable, perhaps, to recognise that at some point my grandparents must have become aware that their role in their son's less-familiar future might be unclear.

Being middle class is one of the things I inherited from my dad which was not passed down from his father. So this letter makes me wonder whether my grandfather may have felt, around the time it was written, that his child might be leaving him behind.

o o o

1 x slim, gold watch

1 x engagement ring, set with a small diamond

1 x plain wedding band

1 x lace tablecloth

o o o

This might be a good time to mention that the word *punctum* can refer not only to the philosophical concept theorised by Barthes, but also to a particular type of physiological blind spot in a person's vision. One of my blind spots has, for a long time, been the question of why exactly I have been so intensely interested in my grandfather's life. It is striking, the way my interest in him is not mirrored by, for instance, a similar attraction to the story of my father's mother.

Part of it is the simple fact of having his stuff: I own very little that belonged to my paternal grandmother besides a wedding ring so small it fits only on my pinkie finger. It occurred to me, too, that there could be some internalised sexism at play, to casually find a man so much more intriguing than a woman. But even if this is true, I don't think either of these factors alone offers sufficient explanation.

Barthes wrote of the punctum as something mutually constituted, that arises from both a photograph and the viewer. It is 'an addition': 'what I add to the photograph and what is nonetheless already there.' It is intensely subjective; a product not only of the image itself but also the viewer's interpretation of it, and the way these two factors come together in a particular time and place.

It wasn't until I was quite far into writing this essay that I realised the fact I'd been so intrigued by my grandfather and his stuff must have said something about me, too. I've wondered, then, what it might be about my grandfather's life that draws me to it, but also what it could be about my own life that causes his story to strike me so deeply. And I circle back, again and again, to this thing I have always known about my grandfather's life: that it ended sadly, with mental illness, and apparent loneliness, and a long decline. I have to admit that I have always assumed these things were somehow related, and worried what the implication of this might be for my own life.

Indeed, I have come to realise it is probably significant that there are a number of these kinds of stories rattling around in my family history. As a kid, I heard not only about my grandfather but also someone who, if memory serves, would have been my great-grandmother. Supposedly she sat down in a chair one day and announced she was never again getting up, and didn't. That's what I was always told.

So here is the point. Mental illness is something that—like the small, brown suitcase—I have inherited from grandfather via my dad. And so, while I have been trying to understand his fate and my father's through the objects in the suitcase, I have also been addressing my own fears about the future.

o o o

The second half of *Camera Lucida* centres around an image known as the Winter Garden Photograph, which depicts Barthes' late mother as a five-year-old. It was, for him, the only picture he found that seemed to capture 'the truth of the face I had loved'—that captured some of the reality of his mother's features, which he'd struggled to summon in his mind 'as a totality' since she had died. In describing this physical evidence of the 'radiant, irreducible core' of who his mother was, Barthes reminds us that he had lost not only a generalised figure ('the Mother'), but also *his* mother, who had 'that grace of being an individual soul'.

Barthes declined to reproduce the Winter Garden Photograph in *Camera Lucida*, although the book includes many of the other images that he references. Some critics have taken this as evidence that the photograph did not actually exist, but Barthes explained himself by saying that, for his readers, it 'would be nothing but an indifferent picture'. 'At most,' he wrote, 'it would interest your studium: period, clothes, photogeny; but in it, for you, no wound.' And yet he could not have possibly known whether or not this was true: the punctum, by definition, is subjective and personal. My suspicion, then, is that Barthes simply wanted to keep this picture—this precious relic of his beloved mother—to himself.

Perhaps this seems contradictory in such an intensely personal book, but I can understand the impulse. It can be difficult to write about these kinds of things, even when the people involved are no longer alive to care about the result. I am always aware of how badly I might be getting it wrong. Writing about other people, actual or imagined, carries the risk that you'll turn them into a poorly drawn character rather than something that resembles a real human being; that you'll flatten them out by favouring one aspect of their being over the others. Doing so for the eyes of others—in the potentially unflattering glare of third-party interpretations—adds to the potential for misunderstanding.

The degree of difficulty is further heightened when you're writing about someone you've encountered only through their things, because you can never know how close your reading of the available clues has come to the truth. I possess these souvenirs of my grandfather's life, but I have little certainty about what they meant to him. I cannot see them in the context in which they existed for him: in his home, on his shelves or his bedside table, arranged according to his habits and fancies. I can view them only as I do: jumbled together, mixed up, in the suitcase.

For Barthes, the punctum of an image was necessarily elusive. Its effect is ambiguous: 'certain but unlocatable'; 'acute yet muffled'; 'a floating flash'. It is 'sharp and yet lands in a vague zone of myself'. Sometimes, he wrote, it is revealed 'only after the fact, when the photograph is no longer in front of me and I think back on it'.

Perhaps, then, it is the not-knowing—the fact that I will never know for sure—that keeps me coming back to the contents of the small, brown suitcase.

o o o

1 x shirt (blue and cream)

2 x cotton turtlenecks (dark blue, brown)

1 x pair slippers

1 x blue cardigan

2 x pairs shoes

1 x grey pants

2 x light brown shirts

o o o

One of the most pointedly affecting items in the suitcase is this list of my grandfather's clothing, made the year after my grandmother died. There are two columns, separated by a few inches of white space, the words 'old' and 'new' printed at the top. Underneath, precisely forty-nine items are catalogued in my dad's restrained hand. This might sound like quite a lot until you consider that this number includes eight pairs of underpants, ten handkerchiefs, six singlets, and a set of slippers.

I can picture my dad, writing this list using one of those rollerball pens he always favoured, its fine tip abrasive against the sheet of lined paper. I can picture it because I have watched him, hunched over a piece of work like this, in the past. And yet I cannot be sure why

Dad might have made this list. My best guess is that he was making sure his father was adequately equipped before he moved into the nursing home. This would have been exactly the kind of thing my dad would have done: not only to have made the list, but to have kept it for decades afterwards, in a folder with his father's death certificate and the cremation receipt, as if he might one day need it all again. (He was a very organised person. That's another thing I have inherited from him.)

When I first came across the list of clothing, I found it unsettling. Something about its matter-of-factness, its sober practicality, seemed to imply a certain sterility, not only in terms of the life it inadvertently encapsulates but also the depth of feeling that might have motivated its drafting. Then I encountered the suggestion, made by author Lulah Ellender, that 'writing a list is a rational act in the face of pure emotion … as if the process of shifting all the complexities from our heads into inky lines makes it all more manageable'. And so I returned to this image of my dad, pen in hand, except now I could picture not only his stooped form but also the deep furrow between his eyebrows and the concentration around his eyes. Could imagine the worry, the sense of being out of his depth, perhaps, in a fast-flowing river of fresh responsibility. And so I began to see the list in a different way: not as a product of emotional barrenness, but of a surfeit; of a tumult in search of its opposing state.

o o o

It occurs to me that this story—about my grandfather, and my father— is in many ways one not only of remembering, but also forgetting. Not only of information that has fallen away over time—street addresses and moments of emotion and the rationales for certain decisions—but also of details and incidents and *things* that the participants in this story have, perhaps, done their best to leave behind.

I've mentioned that details about my dad's past tended to be scarce when I was growing up, but I occasionally got the sense parts of it existed not far below the surface. I remember once, when I was in my early teens, asking Dad about a document I'd found in the brown suitcase. It was a card or maybe a letter from an older member of the extended family—a woman, though I didn't recognise the name—who had written to Dad not only to express her condolences following the untimely death of his mother, but also to berate him for not moving home to be closer to his increasingly fragile father.

I'd been curious about the letter or card or whatever-it-was for the conflict it seemed to suggest, but had been unprepared for the depth of feeling in my dad's voice when he answered my questions: the hurt and anger and bitterness that had continued to exist, just out of sight, many years after the events had taken place. (The woman's words retained, for him, the power to wound.) The details of what he said— most of which I cannot recall clearly—aren't especially important, except to note that Dad felt he'd done his best in the circumstances. What's more interesting to me is what happened next.

At some point after that conversation, I returned the suitcase to Dad, at his request (although I don't recall whether the two events were connected). Later, after he had died and I had retrieved the case from my stepmum, I went through it, curious to re-read the correspondence from the older relative. It was gone. Perhaps it had been misplaced over the years, but I can't help but suspect my dad might have discarded it intentionally, perhaps in the hope—understandable but also poignant—that the painful memory it seemed to encapsulate could similarly be erased.

I'm reminded, too, of another detail that seemed to get lost when I was a child. I'd always assumed that the events of my grandmother's death and my grandfather's breakdown and terminal decline had occurred in relatively quick succession, I suppose in large part because they had always been discussed as if they were closely related. But when I was going through the contents of the suitcase and attempting to put together a sort of timeline of my grandfather's life, I realised that there had, in fact, been eight years between my grandmother's death and his own. And so this assumption I'd picked up—that he'd essentially given up after his wife's death, had fallen to bits without her—no longer felt entirely true. You don't give up but then live for the better part of another decade, especially if you're dealing with grief compounded by mental illness. That takes some getting through.

o o o

Another of the objects in the small, brown suitcase is a packet of old negatives, still in their original paper sleeves. As a child, I'd occasionally held these tannin-dark strips up to the light to glimpse the images they contained, but by the time I started writing this essay, it had been years—decades—since I'd done so. I can't really account for the lack of interest they long held for me, except to say that the absence of a punctum is, at times, as mysterious as its presence. That it can, by definition, be difficult to identify blind spots.

Still, one day during the period when I was thinking about the ambiguity of both the physical traces people leave behind and the stories we tell about them, I found myself holding these negatives against the glow of my laptop. And I realised with a start that there were pictures there I'd never before seen, dating from when my dad was living in the US, not so long before his mother died and around the time he met and married the French woman. I had them scanned and converted into digital files. And though they were filled with faces I did not know in places I did not recognise, seeing them on my screen felt like some small revelation.

Among the images was a series in black and white, showing Dad and the French woman on holiday somewhere in Europe with my grandparents. In one, they are standing in a field, my grandfather holding a bottle of wine like a trophy. In another, he appears to have been caught mid-sentence, his mouth open in a moment of suspended animation.

My favourite, though, is a picture in which my dad and my grandfather stand side by side, leaning against a railing beside a lake or maybe the sea. My dad is a full head taller than his father, who has a cigarette in one hand, his other thrust into his pocket. But this is the thing: they have the same squinting eyes, the same sticking-out ears, the same slouching shoulders. The same expression on their faces: part grimace, part smile; as though tolerating mild discomfort.

I had that photo of my dad and my grandfather printed, and then pinned it up on my wall. And when I look at it now, I can see they stand close but not touching, their shoulders separated by only a few inches of air.

Dear Lucy

Perhaps it is curious that the most enduring friendship of my life has been with someone I've met in person only twice.

We would have been about seven or eight when we got started. I'd written into the pen pals page of a British magazine for little girls—an act, a string of words, that now seems as archaic as the all-white world of midnight feasts in boarding school dorms that the publication itself depicted. Being Australian, and thus possessing a certain antipodean cachet, I received many dozens of replies from other little girls living all over the British Isles. I wrote back to two of them: an English girl, also named Gemma, with whom I quickly lost touch; and Lucy.

We began to volley letters back and forth, back and forth, halfway across the globe. I can't say precisely what they contained, but I can guess at the generalities: stories about our lives, our friends, our siblings, school, our shared interests (ponies, and reading, but mostly ponies). Far easier to access is the feeling of receiving these letters. The faithful checking of the mailbox; the rush at spotting one of Lucy's light-blue airmail envelopes—the ones with the navy-and-red striped border, with her neat handwriting across the front—in among the window-fronted bills and folded-over flyers. As I walked back up the steep driveway, I'd test the envelope between forefinger and thumb, gauging whether there might be a photograph—a bonus— slipped between the thin sheets of notepaper.

Lucy and I always formatted our letters correctly, the way we'd been taught at school—the way I'd been taught, at least—with a lot of blank spaces around the page. Blank space beside the address at the top, beside the date, beside the greeting. Blank space at either end of each line, between each paragraph, between each word. In a way, the blank spaces are as important as the words they surround: the words that comprise a letter would make much less sense without the spaces, although the spaces would make no sense at all without the words. And yet, when I think of those letters, my memory is of pages that seemed almost sodden with neatly printed news and stories and words. Of how we were hungry to share, to narrate our lives.

I wish I still had those letters, stored away somewhere safe. Instead, I have the feeling of receiving them, tucked into the bottom drawer of my memory, and a small cache of objects to accompany it: a photograph or two, a couple of postcards, and an assortment of maps. In this little collection, the maps seem to be the odd things out. Unlike the postcards and some of the photographs, Lucy did not send them to me, nor do they depict one or the both of us in some way. Unlike the postcards and some of the photographs, their connection to our relationship is not immediately apparent.

o o o

Of course, you might say that telling a story—writing a letter—and making a map have quite a lot in common. In *Maps of the Imagination*, Peter Turchi writes at length about the ways the metaphor of map-making can illuminate the process of creating narrative. He writes about cartography and storytelling as modes of discovery, as voyages into the unknown, each subject to false starts and wrong turns, to frustration and exhilaration.

He writes, too, of the blanks that exist within both maps and stories; about how 'the need for selection means every story contains, and is surrounded by blank spaces, some more significant than others'. Each is always, to an extent, about inclusions and omissions. About what you put in, and what you leave out.

'Many would argue that the urge to fill blank spaces is fundamental to the quest for knowledge,' Turchi writes. He mentions how in medieval times, cartographers would fill the blank spaces on their charts with drawings 'of sea serpents, dragons, griffins, hippogriffs, and freakishly exotic people', guided as much by the rumours about what sailors and explorers might find in those places as a decorative impulse—a desire to embellish, to fill the empty spaces; the same desire that might prompt people to seek out those blanks for themselves. 'Omissions, intended or unintended, provoke the imagination,' he adds.

o o o

I suppose it's worth saying what happened to the letters. There was a flood; a slow, seeping thing; undramatic, yet destructive. A couple of inches of muddy water that came in through a ventilation shaft, or perhaps cracks in the walls and failings in the floor: the kind of thing you might not notice until the damage is done. Indeed, by the time we found the mess—lifted the heavy panel in the floor, followed the concrete steps down to the cellar—it was already too late.

A weird thing happens when photographs become waterlogged. Their surface buckles and warps, and their chemicals run together, casting multi-coloured clouds atop the image. The sheets might become tacky and stick together, or mouldy and pulp-like. As far as I know, you can't fix a photograph once this happens. We threw most of them out; lost years in that way. Years of baby faces and first days and candles about to be blown out. Not just photographs, either, but also old postcards and the Christmas decorations I'd made as a kid. Most of my dad's old photos on slide film. Albums and papers and a complete set of luggage. The letters, as well, I think.

o o o

Lucy and I met—properly, in person—a few years after we began writing. My parents and I were in Scotland to visit my mum's relatives, so we drove up the coast to the pretty little town where Lucy, her parents and younger brother lived. I retain a half-remembered impression of the fleeting flash of a large pond from a window, of a sky the colour of a ten-cent coin, and of stepping out of the hire car at a farmhouse just beyond the edge of town. A border collie, the promise of a pony in the paddock with the wooden fence, a bedroom tucked into the eaves of the house, even a little brother to boss about. When I say that I envied all of it—coveted all of it—I don't mean that I was jealous of Lucy or thought her undeserving of this apparent idyll. What I mean is that, like a lot of day-dreamy kids who should know better, I spent a frankly puzzling amount of time wishing I were someone else, and Lucy and her life—my idea of her life—were not excepted from this yearning.

After our visit, we kept writing. I wrote to her when I became an aunt, age thirteen; when pets died; when friendships failed. When I had birthdays; when she did. I wrote to her about all manner of things, mundane and otherwise. But writing to her wasn't like keeping a diary. I glossed things over, left things out: the churn of my teenage emotions, the deep-seated sense of inadequacy and doubt, the shame that accompanied each new eruption or mutation of my adolescent body. I remember trying to make myself sound cooler than I was when I wrote to her about the music I liked and the boys I knew, playing up how I listened to The Beatles now, how I'd spoken to that guy Nick for an hour on the phone the other night, how *he'd* called *me*, not the other way around. Lucy was unique in my life in that she knew almost nothing about me that I hadn't told her myself. And though I wouldn't have lied to her, I could and almost certainly did try to project a better—'better'—version of myself into the gaps in her knowledge.

I suppose there was a similar process at work in reverse. Chalk it up to an absence of empathy or imagination or information or maybe all three, but, at that age, it can be easy to assume that nothing much of significance—certainly nothing bad—plays out in other people's lives when they're absent from the stage set of your own. And so, without really meaning to, I imagined for Lucy an idealised existence based only in part on what she shared with me. I did this so completely, so unconsciously, that I came to think of her as my more successful double: myself had I been smarter and prettier and, later in our teens, been admitted to one of the world's most prestigious universities to study something that seemed far more straightforwardly useful (medicine, like her, rather than literature, like me). That I had much to be grateful for—that, as my mother was fond of reminding me, I should have been counting my very considerable blessings—was apparently beyond me at the time.

It similarly never occurred to me that just as I was smoothing things over and leaving things out, Lucy must have been doing the same. Indeed, it wasn't until many years later that I learnt how, at the time we'd visited her family, one of Lucy's parents had been struggling with serious but invisible health problems. It wasn't until years later still that I heard about some of the ways this period had indelibly imprinted itself on my friend's psyche. That I learnt there had been a gap between the object of my half-formed and fairly innocent envy and the inevitably messier reality.

There's a famous line in the study of cartography, coined by philosopher Alfred Korzybski in the 1930s: the map is not the territory. It calls attention to the fact that any representation of reality is just that: the result of decisions about what to leave in and what to leave out. Just as the map is not identical to the territory it depicts, our lives are not the stories told about them by ourselves and others, even as the former is shaped by the latter and the latter constrained by the former. Stories are surrounded by silences. By omissions that provoke the imagination.

o o o

While I was writing this, I wondered what I should leave out: the stuff about Lucy's parent's health, mostly. I was going to mention the more precise nature of their illness, but that seemed unnecessarily intrusive. I switched to thinking that maybe I could just hint at some unspecified family trouble, some personal struggles, to protect their privacy. But then I remembered the hideous creatures on those medieval maps; the way our minds might fill a blank with the worst thing we can imagine. Lucy is not Lucy's real name—maybe that much was already clear—but I don't want anyone reading this to imagine a situation much worse than the reality. To fill a silence with something monstrous, just as I'd once filled it with fantasy.

I've had doubts about writing this down at all. In her essay 'Holidays with Men', Ellena Savage reflects on an acquaintance recognising themself in something she'd written. She was 'mortified' to have 'exposed this person, who hadn't wronged me in any way, to the awfulness of having been written about'. But she goes on to say that the humiliation of this experience 'is lined with the egoistic delight in being written about'. So perhaps it's not all bad. Still, I have misgivings, even though I could count on one hand the number of people—all of whom are closely related to one or the other of us—who would recognise Lucy from this account. But I also couldn't think of another way to get all of this straight in my head.

o o o

Something began to change for me around my mid to late teens. The best way I can explain it is that I stopped doing things. I stopped playing hockey and swimming competitively and trying to make it onto the interschool athletics team. I stopped going to piano lessons, taught by an older woman whose gentle kindness I shucked off with a blithe teenage disregard. I stopped doing the arts and crafts projects that had occupied long hours on weekends—the mosaics and mixed-media collages and paintings of witchy women with long, windswept hair. I stopped reading certain kinds of books, and watching certain kinds of shows, and wanting to ride horses. Most of what filled these gaps were the things that teenagers usually did at that time: spending hours and hours with friends, and watching movies, and talking on the cordless landline and, later, going to parties and standing around talking and grimacing as we attempted to convince ourselves that we could learn to enjoy beer.

It was around this time that my letters with Lucy began to tail off. There was, as I remember it, a mutual slowing in our correspondence. We might have switched to email for a while, and I still have a few postcards she sent during that period, from a holiday to the US and from the city where she moved for university. Still, I suspect our growing apart was like the flood—slow and seeping, so gradual we wouldn't have noticed until it was up to our ankles.

o o o

Maps, like letters, enable communication across even vast expanses of time and space. Like letters, they have become somewhat outmoded in their physical form. But they remain potent, symbolic, rich with associations. You have to 'read' a map, like you read a story; interpret its scale and key and conventions; work out what its creators have left in and what they've left out; what they're drawing your attention to and what they're obscuring. Perhaps Lucy has been like a map to me, or if not a map then a guidepost; a means to orient myself: she is one of the people I have known the longest, outside my family. I've had trouble keeping track of my thinking on the matter, at times: my thoughts kept going astray. (I'm tempted to say that maybe I needed a map.)

The maps in the little collection of objects that circle my memories of her include a photocopied A4 sheet, black and white and worn along the grooves where it has been folded into quarters. We used it to navigate to Lucy's family's farmhouse when we visited them in Scotland, our route traced in pink highlighter, our destination marked like treasure with an X. There's also the old-fashioned atlas we kept at home when I was a kid, its pages seeming as big as bath towels, on which I inscribed the places familiar from my personal geography, among them the small town where Lucy then lived. The postcard she'd sent me around age eighteen, when she'd first arrived at university, with a photograph of her new home on the front, the buildings shot from above like an intricate, multi-coloured map. The street atlas I'd bought before we met up in London.

There was also the feeling that came after we met up that night, after we saw each other face-to-face, in person, for the second time. I found myself unable to make sense of the situation, quite lost within it. I was disoriented, at a loss what my next step should be.

o o o

Lucy and I were twenty-two, maybe twenty-three, when we arranged to meet in London. We stood there, outside the Tube station at Covent Garden, sneaking glances at each other for five, six, seven minutes until I got cold fingers and brave feet and made the approach. I wasn't expecting your hair to be so short, she'd said. I hadn't been expecting hers to be so blonde. Her voice sounded nothing like how I'd remembered it.

I can tell you that we talked and talked and talked that night, although I can't tell what we talked about—not for some high-minded reason, not for privacy's sake, not because I've resolved to omit something, but because the two bottles of wine we drank in quick succession left behind a blankness in my memory, a smooth surface off which efforts at remembrance bead and slide like rain off a tin roof. I know we had a good time. When I think back on that night, there's a warmth, an afterglow. I think we hugged before we went home.

The next day, we exchanged sincere messages about how great it had been to see one another, and planned to do so again soon. And then, nothing. Nothing for a whole week. I sent Lucy a few more messages and even tried to call, but there was no return text, no call back.

Eight days later, on the night we had intended to meet, my phone buzzed, skittling across the coffee table. She couldn't make it, had to stay late at the hospital; another time? I messaged back, saying of course, that it was fine (how could I argue with the saving of lives?). I received no reply. I tried to call and message and reach her on social media before I left London, but she seemed to have disappeared from my life as swiftly as she re-entered it.

o o o

There's a myth that, on old maps, uncharted waters or unexplored territories were oftentimes labelled with a warning: 'Here be dragons.' However, despite the images of dragons on medieval maps, this phrase seems to have arisen more from literary representation than actual cartographical practice. It's hard to tell exactly what its origins might be.

Maybe it's related to the fact that mapmakers did draw in the dragons—the pictures of sea serpents and griffins and hippogriffs. Chet van Duzer, a cartographical historian, has said this practice may have been partly motivated by the concept of the horror vacui: the fear of an empty space, and the compulsion to embellish it to excess. Perhaps it was also a way to avoid admitting a gap in knowledge, to avoid the anxiety that not-knowing can bring.

But I wonder whether there might be a certain satisfaction in admitting what you are unsure about; in identifying the unknown even as it remains fundamentally mysterious. We might not know exactly what occupies a blank space—on a map, in a story—but it doesn't mean there's nothing there. And knowing what we don't know can also be a form of knowledge.

There's an often-cited short story by Jorge Luis Borges called 'On Exactitude in Science', about an empire whose cartographers made a map 'which coincided point for point with it', depicting it on a one-to-one scale. And yet subsequent generations quickly realised this enormous map was not actually useful: that you couldn't navigate with a chart the same size as the land it depicts. This is a story about the importance of gaps: of leaving things out, of losing detail. About the ways gaps can clarify, rather than confuse; can make things make sense, or make them useful. Can make space for other possibilities, and other stories.

○ ○ ○

Anyone who writes will inevitably ask themself at some point—or probably many—why they are writing about the things they're writing about in the particular way that they are. Such questions take on a heightened tenor when you're writing about your own experiences: who do we think we are, to assume our lives are in any way interesting to other people?

The answer, in my case, may well be that I am an incorrigible narcissist; I'm not well placed to pass judgment on that score. But another possibility might lie with those letters I wrote to Lucy when I was young. Corresponding with her allowed me not just to record my experiences in words, but also to learn to shape them for the eyes of a reader whose goodwill felt blessedly assured.

Indeed, one of the things I was learning back then was to identify the types of stories that people like to be told. This would have factored into my correspondence with Lucy in largely unconscious ways, but I think it would have been more significant in face-to-face interactions, where the feedback you might receive is far more immediate than when you're writing letters and sending them halfway across the globe. Later on, this sense for stories that engage other people's attention would become a key component of my job in journalism, where it's known as 'news sense' and tends to be regarded as a form of intuition which might be developed rather than a skill that can be directly learnt or taught.

One of things I would have been unconsciously taking on board when first writing to Lucy is that we often don't tell stories about things that might have something of the tenor of that flood that destroyed her letters: about slow, gradual things that seem insufficiently dramatic to reliably hold other people's attention. About friendships that ebb and flow in an ordinary and unremarkable fashion, or illnesses that seep into the corners of your life over years, or the objects that occupy our houses, or even bereavements we learn to accommodate over the course of decades. Perhaps we don't think they are important enough to tell; perhaps they can seem to resist the contours of those kinds of stories: the ones with clear and satisfying beginnings, middles, and ends; with neatly defined conflicts and satisfying resolution; that make definite and unambiguous sense. And yet I have found that they can also be a way to try to chart a course through things that feel disorienting or unresolved.

Maybe, then, it was Lucy's letters that were the map, helping me to gain perspective not only on the landscape of my life but also on the stuff of telling stories.

o o o

More than a decade after we'd met in London, I received a letter from Lucy, her first in fifteen years or maybe longer. We'd had some sporadic contact in the meantime—birthday well wishes, mostly; the conversations quickly petering out—but then she messaged me on social media and asked if I might mind if she wrote to me once again. We began to trade letters through the post, just as we had when we were kids.

Though I love receiving her letters, there is no longer that frantic search in the mailbox or the urgent scrabble to reply. I'm tempted to offer this up as proof of the way I've matured, as though Lucy's friendship is a milestone to show how far I've come. But that would be forgetting the ways in which she, too, has changed. Besides which, in a lot of ways, writing to Lucy again feels most like a return: to our friendship, but also to some aspect of an earlier version of myself. (I'm reminded, when I leaf through my items connected to her, of reading that, in French, 'souvenir' is a verb meaning not only 'to remember', but also 'to get back to myself'.)

Indeed, the thing that has really been altered is not so much the two of us as the world around us, and the ways people relate to one another in it. No one writes letters anymore, and it would be much easier, much quicker and more convenient, for us to keep in touch on Facebook or Instagram or via email or WhatsApp or text message or Skype or something else. Some of her more recent letters to me, delayed by the pandemic, took two months to arrive. But there is something about communicating through the mail that I think seems to work well for our friendship.

We tend to think of in-person interactions as somehow better and truer and more authentic than any other way of being in touch, be it low or high tech. But it is clear that the fact Lucy and I forged our relationship through letters has been far more positive than not. Maybe it's the way letters facilitate intimacies and the sharing of confidences rather than the mundane minutiae and rash opinions that more often populate digital channels. Maybe it's the fact that receiving a piece of hand-addressed mail remains a thrill. Or maybe it's that letters, by virtue of being slow and considered beasts, provide a space we find in few other places. I trust Lucy implicitly, but our method of communication means she is at a distance. Perhaps this distance—this gap—facilitates something that was ruptured when we met up as adults in London; something we had to wait for time to reinstate.

It's because of this, I think, that I am still able to tell Lucy things I would tell few others: our letters are mostly about the big stuff, the important stuff, with relatively little said about the day to day. I know her thoughts on marriage and children; her feelings about her job, about the place in the world where she feels most at home, and some of the ways she's sought to make a life for herself. Yet I have no idea what she eats for breakfast; what time she goes to bed; what types of books she reads, or doesn't. I don't really know what her house looks like, or even whether she lives alone or with a housemate or friends. I have her email address, but I hadn't used it in years until we exchanged some messages about this essay, and some of the things that were going on in her life around that time we met up in London. I have no idea what her voice sounds like these days.

Sometimes, we might go for months at a time without writing. Even while I've been working on this essay, there have been ebbs and flows in our correspondence. Periods where letters might follow one another in relatively short succession, followed by gaps of many, many months. Every time I post a letter to Lucy, I'm not entirely sure whether I'll receive a reply, but the uncertainty of that no longer bothers me quite as much as it once did.

The Things We Live With, Part II

'The order that constitutes the experience of home often looks like chaos to an outsider. Indeed, many people are more at home among their own "disorder" than within someone else's "order".' (Kim Dovey)

o o o

It's hard to say what caught my attention first. It might have been the hospital wristband dangling from a wall hook or the map of Florence stuck to the fridge beneath a Willie Nelson magnet. Perhaps it was the old video cameras, or the stuffed toy shaped like an owl, or the head massager that looked like a long-legged copper spider. Maybe it was the ticket for a Bob Dylan concert, or the German phrasebook, or the signed photograph of Janis Joplin. It might even have been the smell: musty, yet almost sweet; the heavy scent of a stranger's home in an unfamiliar neighbourhood of Austin, Texas. There was so much to take in that it was a wonder the little wooden cottage could contain it all.

David looked around, and sniffed loudly. 'It's dusty in here,' he said. The next day, I woke with a blocked nose and the feeling I'd been sleeping in someone else's bed. And I wondered, as I wandered around the poky little cottage on that first morning, what kind of person might have selected that particular shade of bright blue for the walls and those tapestry-style blinds for the windows and the musical instruments scattered around the room—not only the three guitars and the keyboard, but also the bongo drums and the didgeridoo. Certainly not a serious musician, David suggested. 'They're not even nice instruments,' he said.

This game, where you reconstruct an image of a person through the things they have left behind, is one we had played in all kinds of holiday rentals, their owners encountered via email or text but never in person. I've thus become acquainted with getting to know strangers second-hand, with peeking into their lives through the window of their possessions. Some might consider this snooping, but I prefer to think of it as a kind of 'Guess Who' in reverse: you know the name of the person in question, but have to deploy your detective skills to work out the rest.

In this case, David decided right away that our host must be uncoupled, 'Only a single guy would have a house this eccentric,' he said. But I thought otherwise. There were notes from his girlfriend stuffed into the corner of an empty picture frame on one wall alongside a photo of a young couple reclining and gazing into each other's eyes. Pictures of smiling babies on the fridge and a scattering of children's picture books and stuffed toys in the second bedroom. I guessed this had originally been his house, and that she'd moved in. That they must have kids.

Our host's bookshelves gave me a sense of not only his politics (*The Shock Doctrine*; three LBJ biographies) but also his profession (*The Camera Assistant's Manual*; cinematography magazines) and the extent of his travels. The phrasebooks and travel guides (to California, Costa Rica and Spain), along with an entry ticket for the Colosseum and a Japanese dictionary, perhaps suggested a certain restlessness. But I could also see that he was proud of his city: hence the Willie magnet and the biographies and the picture of Joplin, who lived in Austin for a time while attending the University of Texas. I even discovered our host's birthdate, from that hospital wristband, and realised with a start that he was only a month or so older than me.

o o o

Perhaps one reason I was so compelled by the cottage in Austin was that something in its clutter reminded me of my own home, and particularly of the room where I work. Rather than musical instruments and mementoes of hometown heroes, however, that room is characterised by pinboards dense with pictures and postcards; by souvenirs and family photos arranged on the mantlepiece, and—most of all—by books.

There are books squeezed into all the available space on the shelves and arrayed in precarious piles on the floor. Books on the wide desk, and scattered atop the fold-out couch, and underneath it in cardboard boxes. Books in cupboards, and in drawers, and climbing the skirting boards in stacks. Books often escape the room; sprout like mushrooms after rain in messy heaps next to my side of the bed or sneak into the hallway or occupy precious bench space in the kitchen. David likes to say he can tell where I've been in the house by the trail of paperbacks and blunted pencils that I leave in my wake. At other times, he accuses me of trying to keep others out by building a fort of books; occasionally, he just complains—not without cause—about their profusion. ('We're not running a Dymocks.')

Visitors to our house are usually curious about the room, and especially about the books. They tend to pause at the threshold, and then step forward and stoop to browse the covers at the peak of each of the stacks. I often find myself defending the apparent chaos to these people and assuring them that there's a system—if not a precise one—to the arrangement of the shelves and mounds of paper. That I know where to find things, should I need them.

I have wondered, at times, what visitors might infer from my room and my books. Perhaps that, for as long as I can remember, I have made sense of the world through stories. That, at a young age, I became used to hearing incidents from my life, and the lives of people around me, become components of a capacious family lore. That I loved to be read to, and then to read, and write: that the time and space and careful consideration the written word allowed better enabled me to make my meaning clear. That it has seemed to present an opportunity to contain the messiness of experience within familiar shapes.

And yet I worried, too, whether the disorder of this room might be read as evidence of snarled thoughts and emotions; whether it might somehow reveal what I was, at the time we were visiting Austin, carefully attempting to mask. Indeed, while I was poking around in that stranger's house in Texas, one of my closest friends was staying in my home in Perth. And though this person is someone I have known and trusted for fully two-thirds of my life, I'd felt compelled to lock away my notebooks in an old wooden cabinet prior to our departure on the unlikely off-chance she was nosy enough to page through. What might she have discovered from them? In a specific sense, nothing much: they were mostly scribbled notes recording half-baked ideas for short stories and reminders of doctor's appointments and walks with my mum. In a more general sense, though, I feared she would see in their pages clear evidence that I was not coping.

o o o

It was not long after we stayed in the cottage in Austin that my hitherto-reliable narrative impulse began to falter and fail. Soon after we returned from that trip, I saved a document to my laptop with the intention of keeping a diary of my treatment for anxiety and depression. I wrote in it three times that first month, and a final time a short while later. After that, when the document would catch my eye on my desktop each time I sat down at the computer, I would always allow my gaze to gloss over it, knowing that opening it would precipitate nothing more than a confrontation with a blank page and a blinking cursor.

I've since learnt that for people used to making sense of their world in this way, this failure of narrative—of making it, and interpreting it—is a common response to disruption and disorder. Novelist Maria Papas writes of how, when her young daughter was undergoing cancer treatment, she found reading—'an activity that had long brought me comfort'—distressingly difficult. 'I read the same paragraphs again and again,' she recalls. 'I could not concentrate, could not hold in my memory what I had read the day before.' Loss of interest in reading is a frequently reported side effect of depression, and a loss of coherence in the stories people tell about their lives and identities has long been associated with schizophrenia. I found I could still write about other subjects; I kept writing travel stories for the newspaper where I was working, albeit at a somewhat diminished pace. And yet many times, when I attempted to tell someone what was going on, I found it difficult to get the words out, my mouth and mind seeming to freeze in the moment. One morning, I sat across a cafeteria table from a trusted colleague, tears silently streaming down my face as my mouth silently opened and closed as I tried and failed to tell him what had been happening. It felt as if the disorder in my mind was resisting any attempts to render it into language, to wrangle its shape into a familiar form. But looking back, it was more than this, too. It wasn't only that I couldn't find the words to express what I was feeling, but also that I wasn't quite ready to give up pretending I was fine.

Indeed, after coming back from Austin to relieve my friend of her house-sitting duties, she and I returned to the US with an additional travelling companion. I hadn't yet told either of them how I'd been feeling; hadn't wanted to ruin the trip by doing so. I was happy to be there with them, even if, in common with someone with a broken leg or some other injury, I was finding it more difficult than usual to do activities that would not normally have occasioned a second thought. The self-imposed secrecy only made it all the more exhausting. Perhaps this was why, on the plane en route to our destination, I fainted while I was sleeping, which I'd recently been surprised to learn was not only something that could happen to people but also something that had started happening to me. I'd woken up slumped in the aisle, disoriented and surrounded by cabin crew. I think they gave me oxygen. The fainting-in-my-sleep-on-planes thing happened two or three or four or more times around then; it was only later that I realised my body had been trying to speak when my mind and mouth could or would not—that it had tried to signal the strain it was under.

The story I'd told myself about our host in Austin, formulated using the clues offered by his possessions, was convincing in that it made sense of the apparently disparate objects I had found. It allowed them to cohere around the image of a person; made it difficult to imagine any other interpretation. And yet that hospital wristband niggled at me. It seemed to me an unusual item to keep on display. I wondered why our host had been in hospital; whether the wristband had come to represent a triumph over an illness or injury; the reason he might have kept it in a room regularly opened to strangers. I could formulate no satisfying single story that seemed to account for these questions; had no way of knowing the answers.

For a time, I became quite fixated on finding out more about our host than I had been able to piece together through his things. Given that I knew his first name and address, it didn't take much googling to discover his full name, and his girlfriend's. To locate their social media accounts. I could go further: could learn his sibling's name, and his mother's, and his father's. I could easily unearth details about his family history; clues as to the character of his upbringing; information about his career. Could find plenty of photographs of him—even videos in which I could hear him speak. Turning up each new snippet felt exciting, but cumulatively they began to make me queasy.

The amount of information available online began to feel like a deluge in contrast to the more manageable stream in the cottage. I was no longer responding to clues that had been placed in front of me but was actively seeking them out. The invasiveness of that was a different order of magnitude, but this searching online felt different for other reasons, too. In the game of drawing inferences from my host's possessions, I recognised my old compulsion towards story; that urge to make meaning, to interpret, to narrate. To impose order, and turn an experience into prose before it was even over. It hadn't yet occurred to me that I was doing to this stranger something like what I'd needlessly half-worried my house-sitting friend might do to me.

It doesn't, in hindsight, seem like a coincidence that this loss of narrative coherence in my own life occurred in tandem with this search for it in someone else's. But the latter, I was learning, was an unsatisfying substitute. I had no reference against which I could verify my inferences about my host's home; I'd never met the guy and so couldn't judge the truth of my suppositions. The issue in my own life was in some ways the opposite: I had a template for how the story should look, but I couldn't figure out how to make the available components fit; was unsure I even wanted to.

o o o

One of the aspects of my experiences of depression and anxiety that I find most difficult to admit to—more difficult, somehow, than writing about experiencing suicidal ideation, or intrusive thoughts, or even the fact that mental illness is something I will be learning to live with for the rest of my life—is the fact that, around the time I first began admitting I was ill and sought treatment, I was fairly certain I would be better within a year. Never mind that I felt terrible; that I was aware of people in my own life—my father among them—having persisted in the face of such conditions over the course of multiple years and decades; that I have seen friends and family members lose loved ones to mental illness. I was pretty sure twelve months ought to do it.

At some point during those early days, I googled the date for Mental Health Month (it's October). That was good, I thought: I'd have time to get on to the road to recovery, so I could write about my experience and get it published to coincide in the newspaper where I worked. Raising awareness, reducing stigma, all of that. I realise it seems strange to have imagined I would feel comfortable writing about this experience for an audience of hundreds of thousands of people I'd never met when I couldn't bring myself to tell many of the people closest to me about it. This apparent contradiction strikes me as evidence not only of how certain I was that I would be imminently 'cured', but also of the strength of my narrative instinct and the fact it can sometimes feel easier to expose secrets to strangers.

I may be embarrassed to recount the naivete of my past self, and a little perplexed by her inconsistency, but in some ways it's not surprising I thought as I did. My writerly impulse was by then well-honed through years of use. And it was telling me that my experience of disorder and confusion—this thing I feared divulging—might be somehow made orderly and understandable through the imposition of narrative; indeed, not only by making it *mean* but also by making that meaning known. It hadn't yet occurred to me that thinking about my life in this way—as fodder for narrative; as conforming to predetermined arcs; as potential grist for a writerly mill—might have been part of the problem in the first place.

But this is what we're expected to do with illness in general: to find a silver lining, a lesson, a story that makes sense of suffering. Around the time I first started taking antidepressants, I read Barbara Ehrenreich's book *Smile or Die*, in which she writes about her experience of being treated for breast cancer. She is disturbed, during this period, by what she describes as 'the near-universal bright-siding of the disease': the view, encountered in both popular media and online discussion boards, which de-emphasises the condition as a potentially deadly ordeal in favour of framing it as an opportunity for personal and spiritual growth—perhaps even as some perverse 'gift'. She cites a quote from Lance Armstrong, who famously survived testicular cancer and once said that the disease was the best thing that ever happened to him.

This correlates with the way we tend to assume these kinds of stories should go, appearing to bend inexorably towards meaning, and even a cure. There are plenty of problems with this, but Armstrong's words get at one of aspect that particularly bothered me: the way these stories were so often told from an endpoint of redemption and renewal and even recovery, in which ill-health of any type exists as something to 'get over' and move past. It wasn't that I didn't think such an idea was desirable, but that more and more I found I could no longer envisage a clear ending a few months or even a year down the line. It wasn't only that what I was dealing with failed to conform to any familiar logic: that although I was doing all the 'right' things, the treatments and interventions which were supposed to make me better were not reliably helping, or that there was no obvious reason why I might be on the up, relatively speaking, one week and entirely the opposite the next. I was also becoming aware that I was in the midst of this experience. (In many ways, I still am.) To imagine that this state of being might have an upside seemed to deny that feeling how I did was not a viable way to live.

This was the crux of it, I think: a gut rejection of the idea that all of this might, at some point, be 'worth' it; might be somehow redeemed by the lessons I would inevitably take from it. But being unwell isn't a ledger of pros and cons to be neatly balanced. Journalist and author Lucia Osborne-Crowley writes that 'some things don't mean anything, and illness is often one of those things'. 'Sometimes suffering is not profound, and sometimes pain and sadness are not interesting,' she says. 'Sometimes pain is just pain, and illness is just illness, and it is truly as empty and suffocating as that.'

∘ ∘ ∘

In attempting to read my Austin host's home like a book, I'd been operating from the assumption that our possessions should have meaning; should say something about us. I hadn't considered that some of them—the hospital band, for instance—might mislead or misdirect. Just because my host had left some obviously intimate items on display (the love letters), it didn't follow that all the objects in the cottage were similarly freighted with significance. Maybe he'd been briefly admitted to hospital for some relatively routine reason—a broken toe that required the insertion of a pin or, I don't know, sinus surgery— and had casually added the wristband to his collection mostly out of the habit of saving stuff. Maybe there were other possessions, like my notebooks, that he'd hidden from prying eyes.

Perhaps, then, the fact the wristband was on display spoke not to its wealth of meaning but to its lack. Maybe it was less like my notebooks and more like the majority of the books in my house, the ones that are just passing through, sent to me by publicists for my job writing reviews and lingering for a few months before being dispersed to friends or family or a local little free library. Visitors often examine the spines down their sides out of curiosity, but they'd be wrong to think their placement denotes anything other than the reverse order in which the volumes entered my home.

Indeed, I think the most telling characteristic of both my books and my notebooks is not the specifics of the titles themselves or what's written within them, but the ways they exist within their spaces—the ones they're allotted to, and the ones they infiltrate seemingly of their own volition. Not only the notebooks hidden in the cupboard, but also the books and their habit of escaping the shelves and the room where I've attempted to corral them. That might speak to the way stories can seem to resist our attempts at control.

It reminds me of how, not long before I finished working on staff at the newspaper, I was presented with an opportunity to write about my experience of anxiety for the health pages. This might have seemed like a chance to make good on my plan. And yet, after I thought about it, then wrote the piece, then thought about it some more, I decided not to turn it in. I'd begun, by this point, to be more open about my anxiety and depression. But what I'd written felt wrong, in a way I couldn't quite name.

It was only much later that I realised I'd been trying to pour my experiences into a container that did not fit them. To make the kind of story we're used to reading about illness, but not the kind that mapped the contours of my own.

o o o

I've tried to write about our Austin host and my encounter with his home without revealing too much of his identity. I've removed scraps of information about his life and redacted his name; avoided describing what he looks like or any details about his girlfriend. I have also inserted details, or altered them, in the interests of protecting his privacy: misdirected, or misled, in the same way the hospital wristband might have done. (He does not, for example, actually live in Texas.)

I've also tried to write about my experiences of mental illness with some awareness of the privilege I possess in doing so. That I have the choice to reveal this thing about myself or not, and the time and mental space and financial support to write about it in this way. The ability to tell a story, and any kind of expectation it might be heard, as well as sufficient confidence that I won't suffer lasting harm if it is. (Still, I worry about that last bit.)

Perhaps part of recognising all of that involves acknowledging some responsibility towards those concepts I mentioned half-dismissively earlier—raising awareness; reducing stigma—along with the solace that sharing can bring. That day with my colleague, for example, when I eventually managed to assemble a broken string of sentences. With the friend who stayed in my house, who admitted she'd never realised how I'd been feeling. So it was, to varying degrees, with all manner of people from whom I had been attempting—mostly successfully; a perverse point of pride—to keep these experiences hidden. I learnt that words tended to beget more words, and stories more stories. That vulnerability tended to prompt the same in return. I started to hear, often for the first time, about the experiences of people around me who had also been quietly coping or supporting others in similar situations. We compared notes on medications and psychologists and what helped and didn't. But mostly we just listened and talked in turn.

It helped, too, to begin to find stories that felt truer to my experience. Not the same, necessarily, but which shared a common interest in recognising, as Fiona Wright puts it in her essay collection *Small Acts of Disappearance*—about her own experiences with chronic illness—'the complexities of recovering, of making mistakes and slipping backwards, of forgetting and relearning and forgetting again, of compromise and conditionality, or even the incredibly slow, repetitive and exhaustingly mundane nature of the process of getting better'. Which recognise that illness can look and feel dramatic (the racking sobs on the evenings I simply could not stop crying; the flash of panic when I was visited by the sudden and unwelcome thought that I could just veer off the road into the river). But that it could also be small and tedious (the obsessive cleaning of the kitchen pantry on Saturdays when I felt unable to sit still and the compulsive checking of the gas stove which tends to signal, as clearly as anything else, that I'm going through a particularly anxious spell, but also the making sure I'm sticking to routines and going to sleep at a reasonable time and eating in a way that won't make me feel worse). The sense of relief offered by this burgeoning recognition of my own experiences in other people's felt something like when I first learnt that the incessant tension in my chest and brow and brain had a name: a tangible acknowledgement that other people might also feel this way.

Indeed, if I have mostly failed to find comfort in the kinds of redemptive narratives familiar from popular media, I did find some in all of this: that in apparent disorder there seemed to exist, if not order, then something that made sense.

○ ○ ○

It turned out there was a lot I seemingly got wrong about our Austin host. I soon realised, for example, that he did not appear to have children. The photographs on the fridge must have been the kids of friends or family members, and the toys and picture books in the second bedroom for guests. It seemed like a big thing to have been mistaken about, and made me wonder whether the stories I'd told myself to justify poking around in his life have also been misguided. I reassured myself that my intentions were benign; that I had no plans to use this information for ill; even that I was making *art* with it, as if that end would justify every and any means. The stuff, too, often seemed to provide its own ethical get-out-jail card: it wasn't like I'd forced my way into his home; like I'd gone through cupboards or drawers or private places. Our host had decided to leave his possessions on display, and the fact he had done so said something about him, too. (Here I'm reminded of a small child complaining to their parent about a sibling: *'He started it.'*)

It wasn't until I learnt that, like me, our host had lost a parent to cancer at a relatively young age that I decided to stop searching for details about his life. With that specific fact, he became not a character assembled through a collection of stuff but a real person. It suddenly didn't seem right that I could so efficiently find out information like this about someone who had done nothing more than welcome me into his home in exchange for a reasonable nightly rate.

This reminded me of another moment during our stay in Austin, when I'd found what I've come to consider an inevitable feature of any such holiday rental: a locked door, usually a cupboard or wardrobe or even a room that is off-limits to guests. This always set my imagination roaming. But the locked door at the cottage led not to a broom cupboard or a garage or a storage room or a cabinet under the kitchen sink. It was a door from the shared laundry into an extension or connected home at the rear of the cottage. Perhaps where our host lived when the remainder of the property was occupied.

This realisation brought forth new questions. Not only whether he and his family were at home on the other side of the door, but also the circumstances that may have necessitated renting out half their place to strangers (the rising tide of gentrification in many US cities; the precarity of creative careers; the all-too-likely possibility that an unexpected medical bill might ruin you financially in a country where health insurance remains a luxury). I wondered whether the eccentricity of this cottage and its contents suggested its regular inhabitants might slide right back into these familiar spaces once we had returned to our own home.

It reminded me, too, of the locked cupboard where I'd tucked away my notebooks. And I might have been an incorrigible snoop, a borderline creep intent on eavesdropping on a person's life through their things, but even I didn't try to open that laundry door.

On We Go

Our first morning in London, well before dawn. I can feel the chill inside the aerobridge, the cold seeping like stormwater around the windowpanes. We shuffle through immigration and customs and that interminable wait around the luggage carousel, exiting to the forecourt in front of Heathrow terminal five. Noses red, fingers icy, suitcases a life raft at our feet. The light seems uncertain, the sun still low in the sky. It is the first day of the new year.

It's the coldest winter in more than a decade and the weather shows little sign of improving. Every evening brings grave warnings of worse conditions yet to come; every morning, news of cancelled trains, late buses and stalled traffic. People grumble, and go outside, if at all, dressed in padded coats, heavy scarves and expressions of extreme forbearance. It's dark every afternoon by four.

I quickly find, despite the cold, that one of my favourite things is to walk on my own, powered by a single-minded focus to visit some obscure museum or specific shop or just to warm myself with motion. I walk across bridges spanning the Thames and through new favourite parks. I pause at the sight of coins suspended in the frozen fountains in Trafalgar Square and a pink-tinged pelican at the zoo. On the bus, or in our bedroom before setting out, I trace my finger along the routes on my map, trying to envisage where I'll go.

o o o

We had been in London long enough to have acquired a British phone number and an Oyster card but not a properly warm coat or a pair of boots. I'd been finding my way with a printed map whose unwieldy sheets—always in danger of catching the breeze like a flag—might mark me as a tourist, an outsider, as surely as a money belt or the puzzled countenance of a person who'd lost their way. As someone in possession of a burning desire to appear quite the opposite, I was immediately taken with the A-Z street atlas when I spotted it at a department store. Covered in leather the colour of the deep ocean, it looked more like a hardback notebook than a map. Inside, London's wonky, winding streets were transformed into an orderly maze of pink and yellow and green lines, with symbols to distinguish a motorway from a primary route and an A road from a B road, as if I knew the difference. Each page was dense with possibility, a grid of tantalising names rich in romantic potential: Cobble Mews, Walnut Tree Close, Pilgrims Way.

One of the things I liked most about my A-Z was the story I soon heard—though I couldn't say where—about its origins. As the tale is most often told, one evening in 1935 or thereabouts, a young woman named Phyllis Pearsall was travelling from her bedsit flat in central London to a dinner party in the upmarket suburb of Maida Vale. It was autumn, and rainy. Not that politely dispiriting English drizzle, but real rain, falling in heavy sheets that rushes along gutters, that sweeps up debris and clogs drains.

Eager to be on time, Phyllis—it feels only right to call her by her first name—disembarked the bus too soon, at the wrong end of the street. Her clothes and shoes were soon saturated, her umbrella blown inside-out by the wind. She arrived embarrassingly late and indecorously dishevelled. Sarah Hartley's fictionalised biography of Phyllis imagines the moment of her humiliation, as her aristocratic host called for towels while her guest dripped 'quite extensively' on the hallway carpet. It was so difficult to navigate London, another guest sympathised.

This sparked an idea. Phyllis went in search of a current map of the city but found nothing updated since before the war; nothing with an index or the house numbers marked. She resolved to make a map of her own, rising each morning at five, spending eighteen hours a day, seven days a week charting London on foot. By the time she was finished, Phyllis had walked some 3000 miles through 23,000 city streets. (Three thousand miles, 23,000 streets: these are the crucial figures, the magic numbers that arise like an incantation in retellings of this tale.) The result, the *A-Z Street Atlas of London*, was published in 1936. Phyllis was thirty.

She delivered the initial copies herself using a borrowed wheelbarrow, but the A-Z soon became a hit. It sold in the hundreds, the thousands—half a million copies a year by the 1990s. It became one of those brand names—like Hoover, or Velcro, or Band-Aid—that generically encompasses a whole category. Its distinctive visual language has cropped up on souvenir passport covers and jigsaw puzzles and wallpaper and carpet. It's been referenced in artworks; become a plot point in novels. In an episode of the BBC adaptation of Sherlock Holmes, Benedict Cumberbatch's genius-detective stole an A-Z from a pair of tourists to crack a code crucial to solving a series of murders. The criterion for the code's key was that it must be 'a book that everybody'—every Londoner—'would own'.

In the decades since Phyllis died in 1996, aged eighty-nine, many accounts of her life have noted another storied detail: how her long-time motto had been, simply, 'on we go'.

o o o

The story about Phyllis walking 23,000 streets reminds me of how women walking alone, particularly in a strange city, are often advised to move with purpose, to attempt to appear as if we know where we're going even if we don't. This prescription is intended to ensure we don't stand out from the crowd, don't look like an easy target or bring ourselves to the attention of those with nefarious intentions. Perhaps it also provides some confidence to appear at ease and in control, even when we're aimless or lost.

This gets at another thing I liked so much about my A-Z: the sense I had, when I grasped it in my hand, that I held the whole city, fixed and knowable, within its highly portable form. This is the promise maps seem to make. Not only that such a thing is possible, but also that they will make us sure of our place and help us to navigate with something approaching the ease of a person who knows the way.

It also reminds me of a nakedly autobiographical short story I wrote around the time we arrived in London, or maybe later, from the perspective of a young Australian woman living in the city. At one point, my protagonist has a nightmare in which she appears on a television quiz show alongside half a dozen other contestants who all share her name. She quickly realises that each proffered snippet of these women's biographies coincides with hobbies and dreams and interests she has toyed with and given up. Each is a possibility from her past—a decision she might have made differently—spun into fully formed people, their lives alternate and often aspirational versions of her own. As symbolism goes, it isn't especially subtle. But it got at the truth of how I felt at the time.

In one of the story's relatively few fictional elements, my protagonist becomes convinced her boyfriend is cheating on her. (Imagine, the blameless and unsuspecting David, when he first read what I'd written.) He begins staying out late under the guise of work and cancels a planned holiday at the last moment for reasons that don't quite ring true. She accidentally reads a text message sent to him by a colleague, signed with an overfamiliar kiss. She is unwilling to confront him, but finds the uncertainty of not knowing maddening. And so, rather than sitting at home waiting for him each evening with only her doubts for company, she takes to restlessly walking the streets. She quickly finds that her curiosity about the strangers she sees takes her out of herself for a time; that the rhythm of her footsteps helps to slow the pace of her mind. She learns why movement is an evergreen response to uncertainty: that being in motion often helps, at least for a time.

Early morning, a month in. It's my first day at a new job, and I wake with the sense that something is subtly but unmistakably different. I assume it is worry, perhaps a hangover from unsettled dreams. Then I notice that the light leaking through the gap in the curtains seems curiously bright and clear. That the sounds of the city are muffled. I nudge the sleeping form beside me. 'It's snowing!'

Rather, it has snowed, crisp and crunchy and calf deep. The waist-high weeds in the small garden of our share-house, the bare trees in the laneway, the tower-block flats and pebbledash terraces: all are transformed by their brilliant dusting of too-white snow. The television tells us the city's buses have been pulled off the roads, trains brought to a standstill. The Tube is experiencing severe delays. Schools are closed, airports shut. It's the heaviest snowfall south-eastern England has seen in nearly two decades. I email the office. 'Don't worry if you can't make it tomorrow, either,' they say.

Outside, in the laneway, we find our housemates building a snowman. In the street, parked cars are tucked beneath their snowy doona. I have my A-Z in my coat pocket—I don't go anywhere without it—but this morning, we just wander.

We end up at a large park in a more salubrious part of the suburb, where we spend hours throwing snowballs and watching the swans on a lake cluttered with thin sheets of surface ice. We build a snowman of our own, adding small stones for the eyes and mouth and foraged foliage to make a moustache. But I still haven't bought boots, and by the time we're done, my sneakers and two pairs of socks are soaked through to my toes.

o o o

The story about Phyllis Pearsall and the A-Z belongs to the time-honoured journalistic category of 'too good to check'. Perhaps that's why it has been repeated so widely, so credulously, in articles and books and television programs; in a musical based on her life, and in obituaries in newspapers of record.

Various versions exist, differing in their detail if not their spirit: of Phyllis heading to a party in Belgravia, not Maida Vale; of Phyllis going astray on an errand related to her father's cartography business; of Phyllis, an accomplished painter, becoming lost on the way to the home of a portrait subject. At least a few people—including Phyllis's half-brother—are convinced she neither walked every London street to produce her maps nor needed to. They point out that she could far more easily have obtained street plans from local government surveyors and real estate agents, something she does describe in her 1990 book about the history of her business. Both that volume—*From Bedsitter to Household Name*—and her earlier family memoir give her father credit for the idea of the A-Z, if not the name. (Phyllis said he wanted to call it the OK Street Atlas, although that anecdote has also been disputed.) Even the borrowed wheelbarrow Phyllis supposedly used to make her first delivery has been called into question, with some sources insisting that it was, in fact, a handcart.

Phyllis does tend to get the credit—or blame—for the A-Z's origin story, but it's not clear to me how it took on the status of legend. That first street atlas did contain 23,000 index entries, and *From Bedsitter to Household Name* describes its author walking at least some of those streets, mainly to take notes on house numbers, the inclusion of which she claimed (seemingly inaccurately) as an innovation. In a BBC interview from the mid-1980s, when Phyllis was in her late seventies, she describes having 'literally walked down every long road in London' while putting together the first A-Z—no small feat, but not the storied comprehensive survey.

For a while, I was determined to track down the original source of the legend, scouring internet message boards, searching archives, listening to old interviews with Phyllis and reading newspaper articles dating back to the 1960s. And though I found differing versions of the tale offering various tweaks and embellishments, I never came across an instance of Phyllis telling, in her own words, a story that closely resembled the myth. In time, it became increasingly difficult to keep track of how much within this opaque combination of rumour, elaboration and contradiction was verifiably true and how much was exaggeration. My confusion was compounded, no doubt, by the fact that Phyllis's memoirs can be eccentrically, exuberantly difficult to read, filled with dense thickets of dialogue enthusiastically punctuated with ellipses and exclamation marks.

It's not for nothing that Hartley's book lays claim only to offering 'the truth according to Phyllis'. Because the more of her story you hear, the less certain—the more lost—you become.

o o o

In *A Field Guide to Getting Lost*, Rebecca Solnit writes that there are different kinds of lostness. Things can become lost, which is 'about the familiar falling away'. People can get lost, which is 'about the unfamiliar appearing'. 'Either way,' she says, 'there is loss of control.'

Perhaps this is another reason I held so tight to my A-Z. Though there were times my excursions around London took me to places I found frightening—through some dank underpass or along a deserted section of canal—I don't recall ever actually losing my way. This mirrors how I have tended to move through life: with an abundance of caution and pre-planning, convinced that if I could only anticipate every bad thing that might happen, then I might be able to prevent it from occurring. In London, I hadn't yet been diagnosed with an anxiety disorder, but you don't need to look hard to see its influence: the ways anxiety and the unfamiliar and a sense of control—the loss of it, and subsequent attempts to regain it—had become yoked in my mind.

Solnit writes about another kind of lostness: of losing track of time; of 'becoming lost in that other way that isn't about dislocation but about the immersion where everything else falls away'. When I read that, I think of the snowman, and the rosy pelican. The protagonist in my story, locking the front door as she heads out into the cool evening. Of Phyllis, walking the streets, notebook in hand.

o o o

When the weather finally begins to improve, it does so haltingly, its progress unpredictable: warm enough one day to leave my coat at home, then raining the next, and bright but very cold after that. I come to regard the weather forecast as scarcely more reliable than my horoscope and learn to equip myself for every eventuality, layering clothing and stashing umbrellas. It is only in hindsight that I can be certain the weather has turned.

One afternoon, in the midst of all this, I am sitting in St James's Park on my lunch break, the remains of a boxed sandwich beside me on the bench. I am watching two women riding horses on a broad, sandy track at the edge of the park. It is another of those perfect, crystalline moments: the sun on my face just warm enough; the grassy smell of the horses and the sound of their hooves on the ground a reassuring backbeat to the hum of city traffic. The women call to each other and quicken their pace to a canter, the momentum catching the horses' manes.

Later, I will wonder whether I really remembered this scene or simply thought I did because I went on to insert it into my short story. Later, I will realise it probably couldn't have happened quite as I'd recalled— that I must have conflated two memories—because though I did take my lunch break in St James's Park for a time, I would have seen the horses and their riders in nearby Hyde Park, where there are bridle paths and equestrian arenas.

It is similarly difficult to pin down the moment we decide on our next move. I'm not sure there is a single, pivotal conversation about whether to stay in London or go elsewhere so much as a steady, ambulatory progress during which the next step only begins to appear self-evident as the toes of the other foot are leaving the ground. On we go: to Sweden, then Denmark. The Netherlands, then Belgium. France, and Italy, right down to Sicily. We return to London. We continue to America. We go home. I never buy those boots.

o o o

At one point, before the pandemic put paid to my plans, I considered returning to London, to visit libraries where I could review old interviews and perhaps settle the matter of the A-Z origin story. I'd hoped the documents I might find could provide clarity and certainty where the accounts of the people involved seemed only to muddy the waters. That they might lend to a life the same sense of knowability and immutability that a map seems to offer in relation to a city.

I was forgetting, of course, that such a sense is illusory. In common with even the most formulaic paperwork, these charts owe their origins to a human hand and mind, with all the messiness and potential for error that implies. For example, another story long associated with the A-Z—one Phyllis does tell in her memoirs—concerns how the index of its first edition came to be missing Trafalgar Square. It originated with a mishap while she was laboriously alphabetising the index by hand, when the shoebox containing the relevant card fell out of her office window to the street below. 'Fortunately the traffic lights were red,' she recalled in that BBC interview years later. 'I tore down the stairs, picked up all the cards, swept them off the roofs of cars, but of course I couldn't sweep them off the buses. And the buses went by, and one of them bore Trafalgar Square.'

Reading about this sent me back to the pages of my A-Z for the first time in at least a decade. I knew the omission of Trafalgar Square would have been easily remedied in subsequent editions, but I wanted to check mine, just to be sure. I quickly—predictably—became distracted by the traces of my past self within its leaves: the pages I'd turned down to keep my place; the phone numbers and addresses scribbled inside the front cover. I tried to recall what business I'd had on Rutland Street in Knightsbridge or Rathbone Place in Fitzrovia or

Henrietta Street in Covent Garden, all marked on the map with a cross. I thought of the Saturday we'd bought still-warm bread at Broadway Market in Hackney, or the evening we'd ice-skated at a rink bathed in a flush of fuchsia light at Somerset House, the corners of their respective pages neatly folded. The afternoon we'd caught the Tube to North London and walked past the bathing ponds in Hampstead Heath and up to Parliament Hill, the metropolis laid out below us, hazy and humming with life.

It was while I was flipping through my little blue street atlas that I realised this book—the book I was so sure was one of those iconic, instantly recognisable A-Zs—was actually a Philip's Street Atlas of London, produced by an entirely different publishing house. As an error of fact, it wasn't of the scale of the fabrications Phyllis has been accused of concocting. But I wondered if my mistake might share some of its mechanics. Might demonstrate the ways assumption and exaggeration and misremembering can solidify to create a story sufficiently appealing that it's easy to overlook any cracks or inconsistencies in its sparkling surface.

Perhaps something like this happened with the story about Phyllis walking London's streets: maybe time and repeated transmission inflated a relatively modest tale into the oft-repeated legend. Of course, there's also the possibility that the story is true, or that Phyllis made it up entirely. Her family memoir, in particular, is filled with scenes and dialogue that must have been imagined or extrapolated from passed-down recollections, given they occurred well before she was alive to witness them. In any case, it is probably fair to say she was an unreliable narrator, if only because we all are, to a greater or lesser degree. Perhaps, then, that most notorious anecdote about Phyllis's life was simply one of those stories you tell yourself so many times it comes to feel like truth.

o o o

I'm quite certain that writing the story about a young woman very much like myself has affected my memories of my time in London. It has made some details sharper in hindsight; without it, I'm not sure I would have remembered the light leaking around the curtains or the coins frozen in the fountain. I'm also aware that I've not so much recorded my impressions of that time as written a version deliberately warped by the lens of fiction. The stories we tell about our lives are never the whole truth—a representation is only ever partial; the map is not the territory—but this one makes no claims to factuality, despite its resemblance to my experience. And yet it is a distortion that feels fundamentally authentic in hindsight, in the way fictions often can.

I can't be sure, but I suspect Phyllis's motivations for writing about her life were different to mine. In the early sections of *From Bedsitter to Household Name*, she refers to requests from colleagues that she do so; says she wanted to document her success as 'a business woman true to her nature' and pay tribute to the friends who had supported her endeavours. I can make no such claims about my own writing; safe to say no one is clamouring for me to record my experiences. Instead, I think it started out, if unconsciously, as an attempt to exercise control. This is what I was trying to do with that story about the young woman in London: to shape the material of my life and so make sense of the unease I felt at that time. I'm not sure I succeeded. In the story, my protagonist never quite finds the courage to confront her boyfriend, although the truth comes out eventually (her instinct was correct: he was cheating). After that, things trail off. In the end, I left her walking through the city, faced with no decision greater than which street to take at the next intersection.

However, like returning to a familiar place after some years away, revisiting that story and reacquainting myself with its protagonist and the version of myself who created her has offered an opportunity to see how I have changed in the interim. I thought of this recently when talking to a younger colleague about her own plans to move to London. She was nervous about how it all might work out; whether she would find a job, and somewhere to live, and a less literal place for herself in an unfamiliar city. It seemed unlikely that she would navigate using an old-fashioned A-Z: few people require a physical street atlas in the age of Google Maps. But I recognised her mix of excitement and acute uncertainty, not to mention—and perhaps I am projecting here—the underlying anxiety that each choice she might make would represent a shutting down of possibility, rather than a shifting or even an opening up. This is what I thought at that age, when everything seemed so terrifyingly consequential: as if, at any moment, I might take a wrong turn after which I would irretrievably lose my way.

It reminded me, too, of a line I came across in my research, supposedly derived from an interview with Phyllis when she was an elderly woman, although I could never trace the original source. As the story goes, the interviewer asked her whether she still got lost. 'Always, dear,' she replied.

Via del Paradiso

I have heard this story so many times that its beats have come to feel as familiar as the creases of my own palm. Of how my mother came to Australia at age eighteen from her hometown on Scotland's west coast—where her grandparents had migrated from northern Italy shortly after the end of the First World War—on what was planned as a two-year working holiday. How she was supposed to come with a cousin who got cold feet—'very cold feet,' Mum told me, last time I asked her to tell the story—at the last minute. How Mum came alone anyway, arriving in Sydney one early February afternoon wearing a short green print dress with a chain belt ('very fashionable then') and carrying only a small suitcase. Most of the belongings she thought she'd want or need—vinyl records and books and photos and her winter clothes; 'the heavy stuff'—had been packed into a trunk sent separately by ship.

Mum is not sure how long she had been in Sydney when she was notified the trunk had been lost in transit and couldn't be traced. I'd always imagined she accepted the news with her usual equanimity, but when we discussed it, she admitted to missing the LPs the most. 'I had all the Rolling Stones records, from their very first one.' She thought they were stolen; speculated whether this theoretical thief might have been interested in clothes, too. 'Things have value.'

One of the things Mum must have packed in her suitcase, rather than the trunk, is a small Italian-language prayer book, about the size of two decks of cards stacked one atop the other. The cover is inlaid with diamond-shaped panels of mother-of-pearl, their surfaces etched with birds and butterflies and delicate patterns. Its pages are edged with gilt, their text enclosed by an ornate red border. I am a devoutly unreligious person raised by atheists but, as a kid, I imagined this book to be the most valuable object in our home.

o o o

Mine has long been a scattered family. Me and my brother in Perth, Mum down south, my sister in Dallas and then Singapore and then Sydney and Melbourne, my adult niece and her teenage sibling in the suburbs of Hobart. It is many decades since my mum and all of her many siblings have been in the same room—the same country, even—and they and their children have long been dispersed across Australia, Scotland, Canada, England and Italy. My dad's relatives are sufficiently distant that I only know a few of their names. And my siblings' father... suffice to say we're not entirely sure he's still alive.

We are scattered. And yet four generations ago, my mother's family had likely never travelled much further than the big town closest to the hilltop village in north-western Italy where they had lived as peasant farmers for hundreds of years. This rootedness was ruptured by the kinds of economic, political, social and cultural forces that scattered millions of Italians across the globe throughout the twentieth century, the likes of which continue to prompt, or motivate, or force people to leave their homes to seek a new one elsewhere.

I wonder, sometimes, what I inherited from this lineage: the rootedness in place, or the restlessness that followed.

o o o

Mum acquired the prayer book at age fifteen, when her parents sent her from Scotland to Genoa—she always calls it Genova, in the Italian way—to attend a boarding school where her cousin was a day student. Things had been rough at her public high school in Scotland—she matter-of-factly recalls having been attacked a couple of times—and her parents thought she would be better off in Italy, where she could reconnect with her heritage in the main city of the region from which their own parents had migrated some four decades prior.

The school was run by nuns who wore purple habits; Mum had 'given up' religion at the age of seven or eight, having decided after her first communion that her Saturday mornings could be better spent in the reverent dimness of the local cinema rather than the airless confines of the confessional. But language was a bigger issue: although her grandparents conversed in Ligurian dialect among themselves at home, at the time she essentially spoke no Italian and understood only a little more. Despite the presence of her cousin—the same one who would later baulk at accompanying her to Sydney—she was mostly very lonely. She didn't go home for Christmas, but spent her holidays with the nuns in the mountains. One of the younger women among their number—'she was very beautiful'—gave her the prayer book.

By the end of the year, Mum could get by in Italian and could mostly understand her classes; could even read some of the prayer book, written in a formal, slightly archaic mode. When her parents asked her if she wanted to return after the summer, she declined. Within two years, she'd be packing her belongings for Australia.

o o o

'What is restlessness *for*,' asks the poet Carl Phillips. 'Can't it be a condition of being human, and nothing else? *Must* it have a purpose? *Does* it?' He suggests that one way to think about it is 'as a form of ambition'. He writes of the restless among us who, 'unsatisfied with ... the usual explanations, the usual goals for and trappings of a life ... push past the given'. Such people are, he says, 'willing to enter into uncertainty—to take a risk—in order to get to something presumably superior and/or preferable to "the old life".'

This makes me think of what my mum was seeking in leaving Scotland for Australia. Her decision was in part related to specific conflicts with her religious, traditionally minded father—I won't go into that—but I think another part was the frustration that can come with being a member of a family and a community that must, at times, have seemed all-consuming. This can happen in any group of people, the way a shared history can become social shorthand, as those closest to you come to settle on a fixed idea of who they think you are and how you relate to the rest of the group. This can be a great comfort—you don't have to explain yourself—but it can also be limiting. At the very least, there's a risk of being boxed inside a particular version of yourself: the one those familiar with you think they know; the one that fits the space they've made available for you.

For my mother, this role was as the responsible eldest child: the dutiful daughter expected to help care for her ever-growing band of younger siblings, as well as work in the family cafe from age seven, carefully handwashing cups and saucers, and serving behind the counter when she was barely tall enough to see over it. I remember her telling me about hiding in cupboards at home so she could be alone to read a book, and cherishing holidays at her nonni's house in another town with no one to compete for attention. She has often said she thought, for a while, that becoming a nun might appeal, despite her early loss of faith. ('It seemed like a quiet life.')

Her role at home also came with certain expectations for her future. That she would, for example, marry a Scottish-Italian boy and raise some Scottish-Italian children in her hometown. She tells me about her first serious boyfriend, a young man with a similar background and a surname that also stood out. 'My father approved of him, but then he started talking about how his wife would never work—he seemed to have his life mapped out, with me in a supporting role.'

o o o

After Mum left Scotland, her role in the family became something different. At eighteen, she was the first member of her family to come to Australia. And though she'd only planned to stay two years, she would eventually be followed by one of her brothers and his wife, and then her mother and her two youngest siblings. Later, after the house in Scotland had been sold, her father joined them. At one point, five of the six siblings were in Australia.

This thing, where family or other members of a community follow one another to a new country, is often stigmatised, particularly when it relates to people of colour moving from poorer countries to wealthier ones, but less frequently in the case of families like mine, whose heritage is no longer regarded as threatening to the status quo. In Australia, claiming Italian ancestry largely does not carry the sting of being othered or vilified anymore, and while this wasn't always the case, here or in Scotland or elsewhere, by the time my generation came along, conservative politicians and society at large had moved on to new bogeymen. By that time, however, Mum's family had long since scattered like seeds.

Mum moved many times during those years. From Sydney to the west, and then all over the state, through a succession of red-dust mining towns where her husband was pursuing some scheme or other. They were in Kalgoorlie when my sister was born and my nonna came out to visit ('quite a culture shock for her'). At some point, they settled on the outskirts of Perth, where my brother was born. Then my siblings' father took off, and life was upturned for a number of years as Mum dealt with the consequences of his actions. Even after things became more settled, Mum still seemed to move house—reliably, as if on a schedule—every five years or so.

With each new home came a shedding of possessions. 'Each time you move,' she has told me, 'there are things that just won't fit.' Mum has tended to be far more pragmatic than me in this regard: she dislikes clutter and has become notorious in our family for discarding things before their time. My brother, in his late forties, still nurses a grievance regarding her hasty dispatch of his childhood Lego collection. ('I just got fed up with it,' she said when I asked, the rolling of her eyes nearly audible over the phone.) And yet she always hung on to the prayer book.

I remember speaking to her once about her early years in Sydney, where she'd found herself an object of curiosity as a young woman with an unmistakably Italian surname and a distinctively Glasgow-adjacent accent. 'Oh my god, did I get fed up with explaining that. And when you explained it they would want to know why your grandparents went to Scotland, which I didn't really have the answer to.' The accent lingered, but her first marriage quickly rid her of the name. And though she was often irritated by the nosy questions, and felt condescended to as a so-called 'new Australian', at least hers was an identity she could shed to the extent required to head off unwelcome curiosity. That she arrived only a few months before the 1967 referendum on Aboriginal citizenship is a reminder that others are often afforded far fewer opportunities to determine the way people perceive them, although, when I asked, Mum admitted that at the time much of it went over her head. ('I didn't become politically aware until I had children.')

In that same conversation, Mum recalled one of her early jobs in Australia, in the head office of an American multinational. Someone important—'one of the big guys from Ohio'—came to visit and asked her the inevitable question about her name and accent and identity. 'You must be so glad you've left all that behind, honey,' he said, after she explained. I can imagine my mum wondering what on earth he meant by 'all that'; the look she might have given him when he said it. 'People seemed to think they were offering me some kind of salvation.'

o o o

I once read that, historically, cathedrals tended to be designed to impress upon worshippers the might and awe of the god they were built to honour: that their grand scale and feats of design and construction served both a religious and architectural purpose. The prayer book has long felt like some version of this to me, except that every aspect of its materiality seems custom-made to telegraph not grandeur but a jewel-like preciousness.

Perhaps this aura has only been heightened by my awareness that I do not entirely comprehend the object itself: that my Italian is far from fluent, and my knowledge of Catholic traditions uncertain. When I open its clasp and turn to the title page, I see it promises to provide *preghiere per tutti i bisogni spirituali dei divoti Cristiani*: prayers for all the spiritual needs of devout Christians. Its pages offer prayers for the morning and the evening; for a wedding mass and for confession; for holy mass and for preparing for a first communion. And though I often get bogged down in working out, say, what *esame* (exam) might mean in a religious context, I know the book and its contents seem to suggest the shape of a life that a believer might choose to live on— per its title—*la via del paradiso* (the road to paradise, or the way to heaven). Such a life was, in many ways, the one that presented itself to my mum when she was younger. One in which she would learn her morning and evening prayers, and wouldn't quit churchgoing after her first communion. Would go to confession, rather than the cinema, on the weekend. Would marry in the church, and presumably stay married. (I could not, of course, find within the book's pages a prayer for divorce.)

Leafing through the book and running my fingers along the faded lustre of its pages also makes me think of the woman who gave this object to my mother. The beautiful young nun, dressed in purple. I am curious about her: whether she is still alive, still living in a convent (do nuns retire?). Where her home was before she taught at the school. Who gave her the prayer book, who her family was, and what they thought of her decision to enter the sisterhood. Whether it was wholly her decision, or one that was made for her.

I think, too, about my nonna as a young woman: about the futures she dreamt of, and those available to her. Another family story I've long heard is how she'd hoped to study music in London; to play piano professionally, even. I have no real way of judging whether she might have made good on those ambitions in different circumstances, given she was still a teenager when the war began and was drafted to work in a munitions factory. Later, she was able to leave this job to run her family's cafe in the absence of her father and uncle and brother. Like so many Italian-born men in the UK at that time, the older men in her family had been interned as enemy aliens, although many of them—including both my great-grandfathers—had fought on the side of the Allies during the previous war. Her brother, meanwhile, was in the RAF. (Here is a verdict on heritage and ancestry: the older men too Italian to be allowed to remain in the community; the younger sufficiently British to risk death in service to the national cause.)

My nonna was a teenager, too, when her parents gave her a baby grand piano, an instrument that would become, according to Mum, 'the most significant actual object in her entire life'. I can imagine it was a big deal, this acquisition, and not just for the excited young woman. It must have given her parents a moment of pride, to afford such a thing, this symbol that their daughter might have a different and easier kind of life than they had.

Her life was different to theirs, but certainly not easy, despite the improvements in the family's financial circumstances. There was the war, but also the toll of at least seven pregnancies and six children, and working 'like a navvy in the business through her pregnancies, working at home well into the night, sewing clothes, knitting and mending'. Such was the stress that my nonna lost a little more of her hair with each birth; by the time her youngest came along, she was wearing wigs most of the time. The piano was a mainstay. 'When you're playing the piano you have to concentrate on what you're doing,' Mum told me once. 'It was an escape for her. It meant a lot.'

It hadn't been my nonna's idea to come to Australia; my nonno had been excited about the sunshine, the heat, the opportunity—'something presumably superior and/or preferable to "the old life"'—that such a move would surely bring. My grandmother brought the piano with her, presumably at some inconvenience and expense: pianos are less portable than people (and prayer books). I'm not sure whether it was the long journey, or the intense, dry heat of the Perth climate—that's a detail that didn't make it into the family mythology—but the instrument was ruined. This was another story I always heard when I was growing up: 'She always held it against the place.'

o o o

The hand, writes Susan Stewart, is 'the measure of the miniature'. Indeed, I think the fact the prayer book fits snugly within the span of my folded-over fingers is one of the reasons for its longevity; its compact size one of the reasons it has persisted through my mum's successive rounds of moving house and shedding possessions.

When I hold that object in my palm, I'm sometimes reminded of the ways in which women have also been expected to make themselves small to survive, or at least to get by. To diminish our appetites and ambitions and bodies and even the words we use—see the ongoing discourse about the female overuse of 'sorry' in professional contexts—to better fit the spaces made available to us. (I think of my mum, resisting the temptation to give the big boss from Ohio a piece of her mind.)

I also think of Mum telling me once about how, during a conversation regarding their divorce, my dad had abruptly observed how small she was. As a statement of fact, this is entirely true: Mum is five-foot-four, and perhaps even a touch shorter these days. Indeed, I think it was partly the obviousness of the observation that had struck her in that moment, such that she felt compelled to repeat it to her daughter years later. The sense that this person, who had been her partner for some fifteen years, was perhaps seeing her—really seeing her—as if for the first time.

There are a few things to be said about this. Firstly, that I have felt it too, the way you can become habituated to viewing someone in a certain way only for something—a stretch of time apart, for instance—to unexpectedly re-set your perception. Secondly, that Mum also told me how her first husband—my siblings' father; like my dad, a notably tall man—once said a similar thing to her. And thirdly, that Mum has, in all her exuberance and energy, the presence of someone who occupies far more physical space, even if she's sufficiently slight that, when I embrace her, I can clearly feel the ridges of her spine beneath my arm.

o o o

Mum and I went to Genoa once, when I was a child. We stayed with her cousin, and visited the school they'd both attended as teenagers. Some of the women who taught them were still there; still nuns, albeit elderly and dressed in grey. We went, too, to the village where one set of my mother's grandparents had been born. It was and is a beautiful place, albeit somehow melancholy in my recollection: a hilltop encircled by cobbled streets and small squares, from which we peered into the pitch-dark interior of the stone house that had once belonged to our family. I remember seeing a plaque commemorating the heroism of one of my forebears in the First World War; the small but unmistakably precious family chapel attached to the house.

In the decades between her year at boarding school and our visit to Genoa, Mum had lost and then re-learnt Italian. As a teenager, after she'd left Italy, she had stopped exercising those linguistic muscles and found her language skills faded quickly. She'd acquired new knowledge in their place; had gone to secretarial college, and learnt bookkeeping, shorthand, and touch typing. Came to Australia, and learnt that you had to go to a chemist to buy olive oil and that spaghetti could be found at the supermarket only in cans (back then, she never lived in the kind of neighbourhood that had a rare 'continental' grocer). She'd learnt how to care for a baby that was not her sibling, and for a family and a household of her own. It was only twenty years later that she had the opportunity to pick up the thread of her ancestors' mother tongue, when she went to university for the first time, in her late thirties.

It was there that she began to learn more deeply about the history of Italy; started to better understand her grandparents' motivations for leaving. She had known life in the village had been tough: when she'd visited as a young child in the 1950s, bread was still baked weekly in a communal oven, water was still pumped by hand from a well, and the toilet facilities were a pile of straw in the barn beneath the house where the livestock lived. But then her grandfathers had come home from the war—one of them from fighting in the trenches, the other in the cavalry—and found 'the country was in ruins, basically'. In Italy, the immediate aftermath of the First World War was a time of acute economic crisis and political instability: rampant inflation, widespread strikes, looting and riots. I'm unsure of the specific ways this may or may not have affected my family, but it's not hard to imagine hearing, in the midst of such turmoil, about a third-cousin or friend's uncle who had migrated to Scotland and deciding to also try your luck.

'I don't think they would have gone to Scotland with no knowledge of the place; they wouldn't have gone if they hadn't thought life could be improved,' Mum said, when we discussed it. 'They wanted something better for the next generation and they didn't see any hope if they stayed.' It is a pretty standard migrant story, but also another way to think about restlessness: as a frame of mind that, as Phillips writes, views uncertainty 'not as adversary but as opportunity, not as an object of fear but, for better or worse, an object of an all-but-impossible-to-resist fascination'. As a form of optimism, perhaps.

Another thing my mum and I sometimes talk about is whether or not David and I will try to have a child. I am not someone who has greatly yearned for parenthood, at least not yet. But when I have thought about it, I have sometimes worried that, if I have a baby, it will be anxious like me. I have worried that because I exist in the world at a baseline level of nervous anticipation, I would not know how to teach a child to do so in a less fretful fashion. At the very least, I'm sure I would find the unpredictability and loss of control that accompanies parenting to be a challenge.

Sometimes we also talk about how mine was a difficult birth, and how Mum was very unwell with an infection in the aftermath. How later, after we returned home, she experienced a period of postnatal depression. I asked her, once, how she overcame it. I recall that she found it difficult to explain. 'It lifted, eventually.'

This reminds me of a conversation I once had with my psychologist—another that I've had, in some form or other, time and time again over a course of years—in which I said I was worried I would always feel anxious. She was realistic, but also encouraged me not to lose hope: another patient of hers had recently experienced the complete and entirely unexpected relief of her chronic anxiety after she began taking medication for a seemingly unrelated condition. It was important to remain optimistic, she said.

○ ○ ○

I suppose it is clear, at this point, that my mum and I have long had very different relationships to stuff. That where I have always been sentimental about things, she has tended to be far more pragmatic. (I would have kept the Lego.) As a result, while I don't think Mum has wasted much time considering the whereabouts of her trunk since sometime in the late '60s, I've grown up and entered adulthood wondering what happened to it. Whether it ended up at some dead-letter office or sold in an auction. If it was sorted through by some stranger, or remained unopened after Mum had shut its latch the last time. Whether it had ended up in the ocean, or in landfill, or someone's back shed or warehouse.

The lost archive is another typical immigrant story, one that might correlate not only to missing objects but also absent people. I never met my nonni, and though I've always heard stories and seen pictures of them, it's hard not to envisage them through the cliches of old-timeyness; as if jerky newsreel footage and the rapid-talk of broadcasters and sepia-tinged imagery were an accurate or lifelike window into the past. Not so long ago, one of my younger cousins posted in a family Facebook group some familiar photos of our grandparents that she'd colourised and reanimated using an app. It was uncanny, the way their eyelids blinked and pupils shifted, their mouths twitching into a small smile when I pressed play. In the animation of my nonno, his right eye seemed to bulge strangely as he looked to the side, but one of the uncles pronounced it to be 'the image' of his father. And though I found them odd, I did sit there, watching as the videos looped, for quite some time.

Phillips writes of something a little like this when he describes restlessness as a type of perpetual dissatisfaction, an unsettled quality 'that spurs us towards greater achievement, only to have us find, sometimes, that there is no ultimate satisfaction, no resting'. It can thus become 'a state of hauntedness'; 'a form of addiction to what the familiar can never give, namely the challenge of what's unknown'. Reading these lines makes me think of me and my siblings, each of us restless in our own ways. My sister, who has lived not only in Dallas and Singapore and Sydney and Melbourne but also London and Christmas Island and some other places I might be forgetting, and who has moved from Melbourne to Hobart during the time I've been writing this essay. My brother, whose peripatetic thoughts often keep him awake. (We are all bad sleepers.) I feel this quality in the anxiety of my mind and body—in all the ways I have described in these essays—but also in my compulsion to roam through family stories; to ask our mother over and over about her year at the Italian boarding school, about why she came to Australia, about her childhood, and her mother and the songs she played on her ruined piano.

For Phillips, restlessness can also be a wellspring of creativity. 'Poetry,' he writes, 'is the result of a generative restlessness of imagination', a frame of mind in which uncertainties might 'become obsessions to be wrestled with', with the poem serving as 'evidence and record' of our encounter with these uncertainties. The same is true of essays, I think.

o o o

Given my mum's relatively unsentimental attitude to things, and her own early rejection of religion, it might seem curious that she hung on to the prayer book for so many years. That it was one of the very few—perhaps the only—object that persisted from her childhood into my own upbringing. When I asked her about it, she referred to that aura of preciousness I'd picked up on as a kid. 'It's a beautiful thing, and it obviously has some age to it,' she told me. 'It was something that somebody held in their hand and made use of—it was important to somebody. That sense of history and continuity—I didn't have anything like that.'

The prayer book's publication date, printed on the title page, is 1889, and today it shows signs of the decades through which it has endured. Four of the front panels are missing, and when I open the metal clasp, I can see the gilt-edged pages have browned and become spotted with age. Inside the back cover, someone—a small child, maybe me—has scribbled on the textured endpapers in blue pen. Somehow, these signs of damage and disintegration only seem to heighten the sense of its gem-like value.

For a long time, I kept the prayer book in a small box that I'd bought specially. I'd thought that keeping the book out of sight might somehow preserve its emotional lustre. But I wonder, now, whether the opposite might be true. Memories are reimagined and reinscribed in our minds with each recollection; they are simultaneously preserved and altered by being told and re-told. Perhaps this is why, sometimes, when I've held this book in my hands, I've thought of pearls, which must regularly be worn against the skin and thus exposed to its oils to keep them in good condition. If unworn for long periods of time, they begin to dry out; become yellowed and brittle. Like memories, they are porous and more mutable than we often imagine.

One effect of this is that such stories can easily come unmoored from their emotional footings once they enter family folklore and become familiar narratives, rather than actual things that happened to actual people. As a child, I'd slipped into the habit of imagining my mum's year in Italy as somehow romantic. Mum had never hidden how difficult she'd found this time, but I suppose my image of it had been shaped by the jolly depictions of British boarding school life I'd been fond of reading as a kid and even by my own image of our Italian heritage as something intrinsically glamorous, despite the humble nature of our family's origins. Perhaps the presence of the prayer book in our house also played some role. 'I always looked on it as a piece of art,' Mum told me, when I asked her about it for the umpteenth time. 'The beautiful book, and the beautiful language, and the beautiful thought to give it to me.'

o o o

I'd always assumed Mum had known I'd coveted the prayer book, and for that reason had given it to me when I'd moved out of home. But when I phoned her, yet again, to ask, she was not only unsure where the book had ended up ('I don't have it') and how it came to be in my possession ('Did I give to you?'). 'I suppose I was just passing something on,' she said, after we'd straightened it out. 'I didn't really have much to pass on to you; you know, something special.' (This might be a good time to note that another thing my mum is known for in our family is her terrible memory.)

For her part, Mum has lived in her current home for nine years, probably the longest stretch of her adult life that she's stayed in one place. It's tempting to draw conclusions from this—to say that her restlessness has dissipated—but when I think of her, it's still as someone most often in motion. She is always talking her partner into some trip or other, even just to Perth, and is known around her small town as the Woman Who Walks on account of the hours she spends on the trails by the river and in the forest, quite often accompanied by a friend but most frequently alone except for her dog. She retains, too, a roving intellectual curiosity, expressed not only in the way she races through new books and often turns family discussions towards big ideas, but also in her empathy and her interest in other people.

The prayer book, too, has come to a sort of rest, at least for now. It sits not in its special box but on my desk, atop a stack of books. Quite often, I'll pick it up when I'm thinking of something else and turn it over in my hands, running my fingertips across the mother of pearl cover or clipping and unclipping the latch to produce the satisfying click of a mechanical pencil. I like the noise it makes when I thumb the gilt-edge pages, too; that resonant flick that brings forth the scent of closed-off rooms and yellowed paper. Still, it retains a restive quality, if only because it remains stubbornly, insistently enigmatic, at least in part. My Italian is still not fluent enough to read it without frequent reference to a digital dual-language dictionary.

These days, when Mum speaks about her seven-plus decades, she often talks of the sense that she has lived multiple lives in one. Like so many people, she has frequently needed to reinvent herself in response to changing circumstances often outside her control: not only getting through that year in Italy and creating a new life in Australia, but also after my siblings' father abandoned the family, leaving Mum responsible for two kids and the pile of debt he'd left behind. After she met my dad, too, and after they divorced; after she and her current partner retired and moved to the country. The success of her attempts to do so has owed a debt to both grit and good fortune—she often tells me she's the luckiest person in the world—but I wonder, too, if there's a connection between her willingness to let things go, when she has felt it necessary, and her ability to adapt and thus endure. As Virginia Woolf put it, 'a self that goes on changing is a self that goes on living'.

Still, I am aware there are some things that cannot be cast off. Like my mum, I learnt Italian outside the home, at school and then at university. At the latter, I had a professor who'd taught Mum two decades prior. He recognised my surname, and remembered her. He told me that she'd spoken Italian with a Ligurian accent, the same one she'd heard as a child.

Swimming, or Hoping

I came across a bit of ephemera on a semi-defunct app on my phone: a packing list for a trip whose destination I cannot recall.

Sneakers

Warm pants

Warm jumper

Shorts

Books

Bathers

Phone charger

It's a relatively mundane but somewhat contradictory document. Which destination might have required 'warm pants' but also shorts and bathers? Which of these items was actually necessary, and which was more a product of wishful thinking: would I actually be swimming, wherever I was going, or did I just hope that I might?

o o o

Perhaps the most famous literary packing list is the one Joan Didion includes in her essay 'The White Album', from her 1979 collection of the same name. As you'd expect, it's a thing of some elegance, pared back and understated, if also clearly—to my pedant's mind—incomplete. (It includes an entry for 'bra' but not underpants; for a 'house key' but not a purse or wallet.) The list was, Didion writes, 'taped inside my closet door in Hollywood during those years when I was reporting more or less steadily'. She draws attention to 'the deliberate anonymity' of the clothing it itemises: 'in a skirt, a leotard, and stockings, I could pass on either side of the culture'.

I never had a master list like Didion's in the years when I was also travelling and writing for a newspaper, and my lists never aimed to be comprehensive: I tended to write down only the items I thought I might forget to pack. And yet I recognise the impulse. I used to deal with the heightened anxiety that preceded a big assignment by buying clothes I thought would be suitable for the trip (I once spent weeks looking for a coat to wear while travelling somewhere cold, only to return a succession of contenders before I'd even started properly packing my suitcase). All of this wasn't just me being profligate, or compulsive; I was determined to be 'prepared' and to look 'appropriate' in whatever situation an itinerary might throw at me, whether or not I actually felt that way.

You can see Didion asking herself similar questions with her list: who will I need to be? And how can I most convincingly give the appearance of being her?

o o o

Sometimes I come across lists in my phone not of things to pack, but of things I saw or heard or experienced while I was away. This one, I'm fairly certain, is from the day I went to a series of street markets in Hong Kong:

International drivers' permit from 1983

Savings passbooks

Postcards from New Orleans & NYC

Jackie Chan

Communist pics

Cathay planes

'Let's go look for crickets!'

When I was a travel writer, after writing packing lists—on scraps of paper, or in my phone—so that I wouldn't forget things, I'd go away and write down things I'd seen and done and heard so I would remember them.

Something these acts had in common was their relationship to time. Both required me to imagine, from my vantage point of the present, what I'd require at a particular point in the future. In the case of the former, I'd consult my itinerary and weather forecasts and websites to decide whether to pack warm pants or bathers or both. The latter act also implicated an implied future self: which details would she need when she sat down to write?

This reminds me of how, as an anxious child, I was often asked: 'What's the worst that could happen?' The intent on the part of the questioner was invariably to reassure me: that there was no believable future scenario I could dream up that I couldn't cope with; that everything would work out in the end. But the liveliness of my imagination combined with a burgeoning tendency to catastrophise meant this question sounded, to my ear, like an invitation to give free rein to my most vivid imaginings without reference to probability or plausibility. Less like a question, then, than a statement: 'What's the worst ~~that~~ could happen.'

o o o

I remember hearing that you're not supposed to re-read old horo-scopes—it's bad luck, apparently—and these lists feel a bit the same: that we most usually obscure their items by crossing them off as we go suggests they're not intended to persist beyond their initial util-ity. And while we often think of the digital realm as disposable—the online churn through trends and scandals; the built-in obsolescence of so many technological devices—it can, in my experience, have a way of preserving ephemera that would be less likely to persist in physical form.

My packing lists—there are many more of them—are a case in point. Few have survived in hard copy; written-out versions have tended to get crumpled up and thrown in the bin once each of their items has been struck through with a pencil. But my phone is filled with them, even though they are no longer especially or even remotely useful, because it is easier to keep them than to go to the trouble of sorting and deletion.

o o o

Contrary to the numerous articles that have been written about it in various fashion magazines, the most interesting thing about Didion's packing list is not the specifics of its individual items: the idea that, in hewing to her uniform of skirts and jerseys and stockings or by imitating her by carrying a mohair throw and Basis soap and bourbon, a reader might capture some of her much-vaunted glamour for their own. Instead, it's what the list and its existence tell us about who Didion was at this time, and who she wanted to be.

Indeed, 'The White Album' is an essay not only about reporting on the social upheavals of the latter part of the 1960s—on the Manson murders and student strikes and the Black Panthers—but also about the psychological and bodily upheavals its author was experiencing at the time. It famously includes extracts from Didion's psychiatric reports which describe how, despite her outward signs of success, she possessed a 'fundamentally pessimistic, fatalistic, and depressive view of the world around her'; how she'd experienced 'an attack of vertigo, nausea and a feeling she was going to pass out'. (Perhaps it is confirmation bias, but these symptoms sound like acute anxiety to me.)

Didion describes how, during this period, she felt her ability to confidently navigate the world had diminished; as if she were improvising her performance of living when 'everything I had ever been told or had told myself, insisted that the production was never meant to be improvised: I was supposed to have a script, and had mislaid it. I was supposed to hear cues, and no longer did'. Maybe it is no wonder, amid all of this, that Didion's sense of self seems uncertain, even fractured. How to reconcile having been named a 1968 *Los Angeles Times* Woman of the Year, 'along with Mrs Ronald Reagan, the Olympic swimmer Debbie Meyer, and ten other California women who seemed to keep in touch and do good works', with the person described in the psychiatric reports as having 'alienated herself almost entirely from the world of other beings'?

The packing list, and the items it references, is an expression of this. She is split: 'in a skirt, a leotard, and stockings, I could pass on either side of the culture.' This ability to blend in was a hallmark of Didion's authorial persona and a key tool in her writerly arsenal; she had previously written in the preface to *Slouching Towards Bethlehem* that 'my own advantage as a reporter is that I am so physically small, so temperamentally unobtrusive, and so neurotically inarticulate that people tend to forget my presence runs counter to their best interests'. (Although, as cultural critic Hilton Als points out: 'the ability to pass on either side of the culture has less to do with what you wear—although that helps—than with the color of your skin.')

Something in all of this calls to mind that feeling of being a typically insecure teenager, when I'd have trouble deciding what to wear before going somewhere with friends. Sometimes, I would wait to get dressed until I got a glimpse of whoever was picking me up through the front window, and then hurriedly make a final decision in the brief interval before they knocked on the door. Here are these questions—who will I need to be? How can I most convincingly give the appearance of being her?—surfacing once again.

o o o

I've been told that when some people read prose that incorporates lists, they tend to skip over them in the same way many of us are so often tempted to gloss long, indented chunks of quoted text. Part of the issue is that, as scholar Lucie Doležalová notes, we don't so much *read* lists as *use* them. They can be co-opted as a literary form, but they're most often encountered as a tool, a way to organise information.

As such, they're often associated with control. Lists, writes anthropologist Sasha Su-Ling Welland, 'tell us what we are supposed to do and what we have failed to do. They purport to keep us on task.' Lulah Ellender describes 'the act of making a list' as 'an essential way to make sense of the chaos of life'. They promise to make the disorderly less so through the imposition of a simple structure: one item per line, with spaces in between. So it is for Didion, who says her packing list was 'made by someone who prized control, yearned after momentum, someone determined to play her role as if she had the script, heard her cues, knew the narrative'.

And yet another characteristic of a list is the way they so often bring the unrelated and dissimilar into unexpected proximity. ('Like the conjunction *and*, the list joins and separates at the same time,' writes Robert Belknap.) Postcards from New York City and New Orleans might thus bump up against Chinese communist memorabilia and models of Cathay Pacific aeroplanes and a snatch of overheard dialogue about seeking out songbird feed. Warm pants and bathers get jumbled together, as in a suitcase. Writer Brian Dillon suggests that an essay can work in much the same way. 'As if I were packing my suitcase like Didion, I list all the things I want to put in an essay,' he writes. 'I treat the essay as a container because I want to smother the anxiety that comes with writing.'

o o o

For a while, I regularly saw a psychologist who specialised in schema therapy. The idea is that people with certain mental health conditions have developed, as a result of their experiences or personality traits or both, maladaptive schemas; that is, as one of the canonical texts on the subject suggests, 'self-defeating emotional and cognitive patterns that begin early in our development and repeat throughout life'. In this context, schemas 'can be thought of generally as any broad organizing principle for making sense of one's life experience'. They are understood as presenting in a series of categories: people with a 'failure' schema, for example, fundamentally believe they are predetermined to be unsuccessful in their endeavours.

According to my psychologist, my maladaptive schema was 'vulnerability to harm': an 'exaggerated fear that imminent catastrophe will strike at any time and that one will be unable to prevent it'. For some people, such dread might be focused on the fear of a medical emergency or becoming a victim of violent crime. For me, it was always something at once more general and specific, encapsulated in that question I'd misheard as a kid: 'What's the worst that could happen?'

One way I learnt to deal with this faulty conviction—that disaster was always imminent; that I would be unable to prevent it—was to strive to address the only element that seemed as if it might be within my control. I thus formed the habit—almost a compulsion—of continually troubleshooting potential problems before they arose. I would list them in my head and pre-plan how I might deal with them. I suppose my belief was that this perpetually looming worst thing could be avoided only if I remained perennially alert to the potential dangers. Such anticipatory anxiety is not an uncommon symptom of generalised anxiety disorder, and it led me towards some fairly absurd mental calculations. (I remember, for example, when I told my GP that

I'd been experiencing suicidal ideation, one of her primary concerns was to establish that, though I was having these thoughts, I wasn't planning how I might act on them. I wasn't, but I was also slightly confounded because *making a plan is what I do*.)

It's not difficult to see the potential evolutionary utility of such hyper-vigilance at earlier stages in human history: anxiety can be seen, as I've mentioned previously, as a faulty fight or flight response that can not only jam in the 'on' position but can also become spectacularly out of sync with the character and scale of threats likely to be encountered in my objectively cushy inner-suburban life. Either way, it made me not only an inveterate maker of lists, but also someone continually casting my mind ahead through a catastrophising lens. There were upsides to this—it meant I have been a diligent and detail-oriented employee in various workplaces; that I am extremely well organised in general—but it also meant I became habituated to living in a constant state of anxious anticipation, of waiting for something bad to happen. Of preparation, and preparedness: in a mode that felt, albeit by a quite different order of degrees, a little like packing.

Eventually, for me, such thinking began to take on a slightly mystical tenor. At some point, I started to half-believe—in the kind of way you never express or even quite admit to yourself at the time—that the act of imagining these worst things was in itself somehow protective. It wasn't just that I wanted to be ready for such eventualities, but that I felt I could prevent them simply by anticipating them; as if thoughts could, in themselves, be some kind of charm or talisman. As if I might think my way out of anxiety when I knew, as my psychologist had told me more than once, that this wasn't how all of this worked.

I'd found myself falling into a similar-but-different type of magical thinking many years earlier, during a period when, in my pre-teens, I temporarily suspected I might have some kind of psychic ability. It was a time when spontaneous predictions about the future sometimes came into my brain, and sometimes turned out to be true. The example I remember most distinctly concerns the end of my parents' marriage. I'd read in some women's magazine that one sign of relationship trouble was that the man—the lens here was decidedly heteronorma-tive—might abruptly change their behaviour in subtle but significant ways. The example it gave was of a person taking a sudden interest in buying new clothes when they had never previously done so. I was reminded of this not long afterwards when someone—my mum, I guess—noted how, in an uncharacteristic display, my dad had recently acquired of his own volition a good number of new shirts. I thought nothing more of it until my parents sat me down one Saturday morning to inform me that they were getting divorced. Despite my supposed clairvoyance, I was caught entirely off-guard by the news.

o o o

Back when I was seeing the schema-therapy psychologist, she would sometimes set me little homework tasks. Often these would involve making a list of one kind or another.

How I was feeling

The things I felt grateful for

My values and goals

Positive qualities about myself

I'm sure there was a specific rationale behind each of these sugges-tions; I certainly found the last one exquisitely embarrassing, even knowing that no one else would ever read it. But the thing I notice now is their shared temporality: the way they were each, for the most part, focused on inhabiting and describing the present moment. This was something I found distinctly uncomfortable at that point in time—I still do, honestly—and was something I often sought to distract myself from by keeping myself relentlessly occupied (this same psychologist once gently suggested I might be 'addicted to housework').

This reminds me of how I have sometimes heard people describe depression as being stuck in the past, and anxiety in the future. This sounds good, but I'm not sure it's quite true, at least for me. Anxiety as I have experienced it has quite often been as much about ruminating over past events as the uncertainties of the future, while depression has most frequently felt like being stuck in a long, glutinous present from which there appears to be no reprieve. In such moments, some-times the best—just about the only—thing to do has been to breathe in and out, and to notice time passing.

This also reminds me of Didion, who writes that her packing list has 'one significant omission, one article I needed and never had: a watch'. As a result, alone in motel rooms at night, she would need to call the front desk—as often as 'every half hour or so'—to check the time. 'Finally, embarrassed to ask again, I would call Los Angeles and ask my husband.' On these trips, Didion writes, she thus had almost every material item she needed—'skirts, jerseys, leotard, pullover'; the list goes on—but she didn't know the time. 'This may be a parable,' she says, 'either of my life as a reporter during this period or of the period itself.'

I'm sure I am far from alone in seeing something melancholy in this scene: the image of Didion, fretful and embarrassed, phoning her hus-band just to ask the time. Dillon describes Didion's packing list as 'one of the most affecting and effective lists I know', but he also suggests that 'the omission of the watch, though not deliberate, appears to have been an advantage'. He writes that 'the bonus of a partial list ... would be that it leaves something to be desired'.

o o o

Earlier in the writing of this collection, a friend suggested to me that a person might read what I have written about anxiety and depression and wonder *why is this person like this?* My initial, private reaction was irritation: does anyone ask someone with cancer, or diabetes, why they have cancer, or diabetes? Unfortunately, I think they often do, in more or less direct ways. Moreover, it's a question I have quite often asked myself.

Didion connects her own anxiety with the time and place in which she is living, albeit in the somewhat vague and ambiguous way that often typifies her writing from this period. She suggests it is an appropriate response to the 'demented and seductive vortical tension' that was building in the Los Angeles of the late '60s, 'a time when the dogs barked every night and the moon was always full'. And though I'm aware that members of every generation since perhaps the Industrial Revolution and possibly before has deemed theirs to be the 'age of anxiety', our own seems to have plenty of barking dogs and full moons of its own.

I can't count how many articles I've read, for example, about how our phones are making us anxious, and social media, and what we eat, and not spending enough time in nature. About historical underdiagnosis and a growing openness around discussions of anxiety and other mental health conditions, and how that can vary across different populations. But also about climate dread and political polarisation and the psychological impacts of the pandemic and 'millennial snowflakes' and the seemingly incessant stream of bad news alongside how much information we're constantly consuming. About the mental load and the ways people of different genders and races and ethnicities and sexual identities learn to exist in our current system and the precarity of neoliberal capitalism and its crushing forms of overt and covert oppression and a society built on relentlessly individualistic notions of 'success' that encourage us to equate self-worth with productivity and ask why we are ill as if it is our own fault.

It's not that such considerations aren't vitally important or useful or necessary, at either a personal or a broader level. Indeed, there are more than a few researchers and medical professionals who believe we are doing ourselves a serious disservice when we attempt to locate the source of our distress solely within ourselves. ('If a plant were wilting we wouldn't diagnose it with "wilting-plant syndrome",' writes poet and clinical psychologist Sanah Ahsan, 'we would change its conditions.') It's more that, like all the other explanations I've heard and come up with—about heredity and genetics and some specific life experiences I've had and the way I was raised and some particular aspects of my personality—none feels especially satisfying on its own. They feel most true and accurate and helpful when considered in concert with one another.

Thinking of this made me think of the way Didion, in 'The White Album', appears to struggle to locate herself within time; a sense encapsulated by the absent watch. I think this failure or inability to locate herself within a broader context gives rise, at least in part, to some of the criticisms of Didion's writing. Indeed, novelist and essayist Elaine Castillo views Didion's omission of the watch from her list not a 'bonus', like Dillon, but as 'a marvellously Carrie Bradshaw-like self-own passing as a flex', representative of 'an unwittingly hopeful, luxurious, American approach to history' that fails to attempt to acknowledge or wrestle with the complexities of the past (clearly this is not a uniquely American approach). Castillo argues that Didion exemplifies this in a neglect of perspectives other than her own in, for example, her writing about Hawai'i. (In reference to Didion's representation of the islands in her 1966 essay 'Letter from Paradise, 21° 19' N., 157° 52' W', Castillo says: 'to hear Didion tell the story, you would never know ... that anyone lived in Hawai'i at all before that great-grandfather of hers came as a missionary (to whom?) in 1842'.)

This makes me think of another thing about lists: the way they can elude their own constructedness even as they draw attention to themselves by standing out on the page. The way they make claims to seeming authoritative and somehow complete, but never are, no matter how exhaustive they might appear.

o o o

Once I started looking, it became apparent that there are very few paragraphs in 'The White Album' that do not incorporate some kind of list. The list of women named the *Los Angeles Times*'s Women of the Year in 1968 alongside Didion, and the psychiatric tests she underwent at an outpatient clinic in Santa Monica shortly afterwards, but also a list of fellow residents in what an acquaintance describes as her 'senseless-killing neighbourhood' in Los Angeles ('rock-and-roll bands, therapy groups, very old women'). Of people murdered by Charles Manson's followers; of the reporters, including herself, allowed to visit Huey Newton in jail one particular spring day; of the battery of tests she underwent before receiving 'an exclusionary diagnosis' of multiple sclerosis. They suggest a person overwhelmed: by information, by detail, by a sheer accretion of *things occurring*. They also suggest someone attempting to put it all into some kind of order, as if the structure provided by a list might reveal the meaning—the connection between the essay's fragments—that Didion is straining to locate. Like a list, the essay's logic is associative, bringing individual items into proximity even as it separates them out. One thing follows another, without any clear sense of how or why each might give rise to the next.

Didion recalls, for example, buying a dress on the morning JFK was assassinated, which sets off a train of thought that travels via a spilled glass of wine and Roman Polanski to Sharon Tate and picking out a dress for Linda Kasabian ahead of her testimony about Tate's murder by Manson's followers at Polanski's home. Some of these details are quite bizarre; it's difficult to be certain precisely why Didion came to be shopping for Kasabian or what she might have thought about doing so. (This might suggest an accusation levelled not-infrequently at Didion: that her prose is not cool or elegant, but evasive or aloof.) But it seems she has the sense it's all somehow related, even if she cannot quite say what it might mean.

The period covered in 'The White Album' is one when, Didion writes, 'I began to doubt the premises of all the stories I had ever told myself'— among them, the Ur-narrative of the writer's life, encapsulated by the essay's famous-to-the-point-of-cliche opening statement about telling ourselves stories in order to live. This line is much quoted and frequently misinterpreted: as writer Emily Carmichael notes, it is often deployed 'as a battlecry', an affirmation: '*If stories are survival,* then *we must cling to them!* we hear her say. *We must pursue them relentlessly, catch them by the throat!'* And yet, Carmichael observes, 'this is not what Didion meant at all'. 'We tell ourselves stories in order to live,' Didion writes. 'Or at least we do for a while,' begins the following paragraph.

Making meaning by forging connections is the way Didion has learnt to move through the world, but in the midst of personal and cultural tumult, she finds it failing her. 'I was meant to know the plot, but all I knew was what I saw,' she writes, 'flash pictures in variable sequence, images with no "meaning" beyond their temporary arrangement, not a movie but a cutting-room experience.' Narrating is supposed to make it all make sense; to give the impression there is some broader logic at play; corral experience into something that looks less like a collection of fragments—'disparate images' making up 'the shifting phantasmagoria which is our actual experience'—and more like something that coheres to form a meaningful life. Without a plot, a narrative, a script, things appear random and unpredictable; we lose the sense we have any real chance of knowing what's next. Life is revealed to be not a series of stories but a parade of unconnected and unrelated events on to which we attempt to impose some sense of connection and relatedness. The Didion of the late '60s, who claims to adhere to dice theory and 'wanted still to believe in the narrative and in the narrative's intelligibility', struggles against this notion. And yet the authorial Didion—the Didion looking back a decade later as she writes her essay—seems to view whatever meaning she might make or find amid those disparate images to be almost a matter of chance. 'One could change the sense with every cut,' she writes. 'We interpret what we see, select the most workable of the multiple choices.'

○ ○ ○

My temporary belief in my psychic potential coincided with what I'd describe as a relatively brief but fairly intense early teenage witchy phase. During this period, I experimented with purple hair dye and low-stakes spells. I spent an embarrassing amount of time in my darkened bedroom staring at the flame of a candle, trying to convince myself I could manipulate it—make it flicker, or grow—having read that the ability to do so was related to the future-sight I was so keen to cultivate.

In those years, I also became a dedicated reader of horoscopes. It wasn't just that I liked the way they promised to predict the future— although I did like that—but also the sense there was some logic, some external order to things. I appreciated, for example, the confidence with which various magazines and websites would present descriptions of each sign: lists of tenuously associated characteristics and qualities which stated that confidence was the natural attribute of Leos and organisation the metier of a Virgo. There was not only an explanatory quality to these lists ('this is why you are how you are') but also an instructional one ('this is how you should be').

This was comforting: the sense I wasn't merely painfully sensitive and, at times, embarrassingly emotional—prone to bursting into tears not only when I was upset but also when I was angry or frustrated or overwhelmed—but simply a Pisces predisposed to feeling things deeply. Not a know-it-all, or prone to moodiness, but demonstrating the intuition and mutability typical of my sign. Not awkward and shy, but displaying a water sign's propensity to get lost in one's imagination, subject to celestial forces beyond my control.

o o o

Work dresses

BOOTS

Leather jacket

Loafers

Pyjama pants

Exercise shorts

I'm unsure what urgency required the capitalisation of 'boots'. The destination, once again, is a mystery.

∘ ∘ ∘

When I read these packing lists, I can see the person who wrote them but also the selves she envisaged going on the trips she was preparing for and the versions who actually did so. It occurs to me that a past self or selves also hovered at my elbow when I wrote these records of things to pack and things to remember. She had learnt through experience to always make sure she had enough of her medications to last the full trip plus a little more and to never go away without a pair of rubber thongs, just in case. She also knew her future self would want to know not only what, for example, a tour guide had said, but also the correct spelling of their name and that of the company they worked for. That she should ask for permission to take their photo, because a past self had been told she didn't file enough pictures with people in them. (I'm reminded, too, of Didion's line, from 'On Keeping a Notebook', about the importance of keeping 'on nodding terms with the people we used to be'.) In this collating of selves, my lists seem to compress time.

One of the things I find most fascinating about objects is the way they do something similar. When I hold, say, a souvenir magnet in my hand, I am brought into contact not only with the self who bought that object and brought it home and chose a spot for it on the fridge, but also the selves whose eyes have swept over it each day in the kitchen and been reminded of the time and place from whence it came. In holding on to it, too, I've come into contact with a future self who, I imagine, will want to continue to be reminded of those memories, of those selves, as she looks back through the accumulated clutter of time and experience.

We often refer to our pasts—and the people we have been—using the metaphor of baggage. They can be this, often enough: a weight, a load, a strain; something to be overcome or worked through, whether in a personal or a broader, cultural sense. But a piece of baggage can also contain things we might need in the future. It's for this reason that the novelist and memoirist Penelope Lively describes memory as 'the great sustaining ballast': something that can not only weigh us down but also provide stability in rough seas. 'The mind needs its tether in time,' she writes. 'It must know where it is—in the perpetual slide of the present, with the ballast of what has been and the hazard of what is to come.'

o o o

Lively mentions another metaphor for memory, courtesy of the poet and essayist Joseph Brodsky, who thought it 'a substitute for the tail that we lost for good in the happy process of evolution' in the sense that 'it directs our movements'.

This is what writer and psychological researcher Charles Fernyhough means when he describes memory as 'Janus-faced, looking both to the past and the future'. He cites a growing body of evidence that demonstrates links between our ability to recall the past and to imagine the future; studies that show how similar systems in the brain are stimulated when engaging in either of these activities. They suggest that people who have difficulty recalling the past (due to amnesia, say) may be less able to vividly envisage future scenarios. 'An ability to recall the past might only be a fortunate by-product of our evolution of a memory system,' Fernyhough writes. 'Its greater value, during our descent as a species, might have been its ability to foretell the future.'

This is less mystical than it might sound. Fernyhough gives the relatively mundane example of preparing for a public speaking engagement: although parts of the forthcoming event may be unfamiliar to him, many elements will be familiar from previous, similar experiences (the venue, or the topic, or simply the knowledge of what it is like to speak before an audience). Thus, the workings of his memory will provide 'a pretty good idea about how such things go, what sorts of challenges I need to prepare for, how I can plan my timekeeping, and so on'.

And yet, as Lively further observes, we not only remember but also 'forget—we forget majestically—and that seems to be an essential part of memory's function'. Lewis Hyde writes about this in *A Primer for Forgetting*, a book he describes as 'a thought experiment' that 'seeks to test the proposition that forgetfulness can be more useful than memory or, at the very least, that memory functions best in tandem with forgetting'. As he points out, 'every act of memory is an act of forgetting', the two existing less as two sides to a single coin than as forces that are intimately intertwined.

If memory is an exercise in narrative, and each story is a representation rather than a straightforward reflection of reality—something that, like a list, is always leaving things out—then it holds true that remembering must involve some kind of winnowing of experience and perception. There are clearly limits to the utility of forgetting at both an individual and societal level, and many instances in which it functions for ill rather than good—to work to erase remembrance of injustice and wrongdoing, and thus prop up destructive and discriminatory systems and institutions, as both Hyde's book and Castillo's critique of Didion make clear. And yet, it is also true that, as historian of psychology Douwe Draaisma writes, 'the absence of forgetting would not create an improved memory but instead a growing confusion', as suggested by the overwhelmed quality of Didion's lists, with their sense of having simultaneously too much information and not enough.

All of which is to say, in regard to my packing lists, that it is probably a good thing the physical versions, if not their digital counterparts, have tended to fall away over time. As Edmund de Waal writes in *The Hare with Amber Eyes*, 'losing things can sometimes gain you a space in which to live'.

o o o

As I was reacquainting myself with schema therapy while writing this essay, I was reminded of a particular section of 'The White Album', in which Didion describes one of her most potent anxieties, which was centred on her fears for her safety living in that 'senseless-killing neighbourhood'. Here and throughout the essay, the figure of the stranger at the door comes, as literary scholar Franny Nudelman notes, to embody Didion's dread as she references the Manson murders and the killing of the silent movie star Ramon Novarro—'not too far from my house in Hollywood'—along with the strangers who show up on her street and, sometimes, 'just opened the door and walked in'.

Didion appears simultaneously paranoid and nonchalant in the face of such intrusions; after a conversation with a babysitter who sees 'death in her aura', she falls asleep in the living room with the French windows open. As such, Didion's main line of defence against these shadowy strangers is noting down their licence-plate numbers before they leave. 'It seems to me now that during those years I was always writing down the licence numbers of panel trucks, panel trucks circling the block, panel trucks parked across the street, panel trucks idling at the intersection,' she reflects. 'I put these licence numbers in the dressing-table drawer where they could be found by the police when the time came.'

There is something of the ritual to this repeated action, in which the noted-down numbers became a kind of list, albeit one confined within a drawer rather than a single document. This is a container of a different and less ordered type, in which snippets of information might tumble together as in a half-empty suitcase. Perhaps this is partly why Didion is under no illusion that depositing these physical manifestations of her fear will keep her safe. ('That the time would come I never doubted, at least not in the inaccessible places of the mind where I seemed more and more to be living,' she writes). Instead, her hope is that this sort-of-list might help someone else to make sense of her seemingly inevitable and grisly fate.

o o o

That a list seems to project a certain sense of authority can, as I've alluded, be problematic, but it can also impart a potent appeal. Lists 'tell us what we are supposed to do and what we have failed to do'. They do not care—if 'care' is the right word, and it is not—that I don't remember why I capitalised 'boots' or needed warm pants *and* bathers. They simply tell me to pack both; to bring BOOTS.

When we make a list, we hope some of its certainty will rub off on to us. Things look more definite, more legitimate when they're written down, sometimes deceptively so. (I learnt this the hard way when I was a journalist.) And yet, though lists appear authoritative, they always leave spaces—literal or otherwise—even if only in the contextual clues we might need to make sense of them (bathers *and* warm pants?). Dillon suggests that a list, 'if it's doing its job, always leaves something to be invented or recalled, something forgotten in the moment of its making'. These gaps can elide important context. But—without equating the two, or suggesting that one somehow cancels out the other—I note that Dillon argues they might also have positive potentials.

This reminds me of a conversation I had with another psychologist— not the schema-therapy one—about my entirely-out-of-proportion anxiety at the prospect of attending the kind of routine but somewhat socially daunting professional event that sometimes still gives me a lot of grief. She suggested that one way to deal with my nerves was not to ignore or deny them, but to acknowledge my anxiety, even speak to it as if it were a tangible, living thing. She suggested I might tell it that it could come to the event in question, but it would need to remain in my handbag for the duration. The idea initially struck me as absurd, even childish; perhaps it also made me feel a little bit sad and frustrated that I had to do this kind of thing to get myself along to the kind of function most of my colleagues seemed to take in their stride. (Here, too, another gap; an assumption masquerading as knowledge.) But the psychologist suggested I give it a go right there in our appointment, so I was obliged to try.

The effect, I found, was twofold. It made my anxiety seem less author-itative, even slightly ridiculous. As if it were an adorably recalcitrant toddler, or one of those fuzzy, goggle-eyed cartoon creatures often used to represent germs in advertisements for cold-and-flu medication. It also made the sensation of my anxiety—the feeling, as someone I love once put it, of having bees inside your body—seem as if it existed at an ever-so-slight remove.

The effect, then, was to open a small gap between the experience of the anxiety and the self experiencing it. A space in which to live, and a way to make carrying this thing more manageable.

o o o

If 'The White Album' is ostensibly about the failure of storytelling to make sense of the rabble of experience, it is also about the stickiness, the apparent inexorability, of narrative forms. Didion ends the essay with another chain of associations that sweeps up many of the figures she has previously mentioned: Jim Morrison and Linda Kasabian and Eldridge Cleaver and 'the fact that Roman Polanski and I are godparents to the same child'. She concludes that 'writing has not yet helped me to see what it means'—and by 'it' she means the items in this list and the ways they are related, but also the period of her life she is writing about and the physical and psychological turmoil she has experienced.

Of course, by arranging her fragments as she does, Didion does make meaning from them—however provisional or incomplete it might be—and invites readers to do the same. Indeed, one of the interesting things about reading Didion is the at-times wildly divergent ways people have tended to interpret her work (so much so that doing so has occasionally reminded me of researching the life of Phyllis Pearsall, in the disorientation it has tended to elicit). 'The White Album' in particular has been subject to many, sometimes contradictory, readings since it was first published. Not only in the example of its famous first line, but also the critics and readers who have seen in it an expression of mid-twentieth-century anxieties about nuclear warfare, a response to the fragmentation of American public life, an evocation of the symptoms of Didion's MS, a critique of 'patriarchal structures of thought and meaning', and other things besides.

Each of these interpretations is grounded, at least in part, in the subjectivity of the individual reader, sometimes in ways they make explicit. Carmichael, for example, encountered 'The White Album' around the time her doctors were investigating whether she, too, might have MS. In her analysis of the essay as an expression of mid-twentieth-century nuclear anxiety, Nudelman acknowledges that, as a graduate student in California reading the piece for the first time in the late '70s, she recognised its 'figure of the stranger at the door as a metaphor for nuclear destruction only because a sense of nuclear danger was a constant' in her own life. Such responses are sometimes a litmus test of individual views of Didion: writer Caitlin Flanagan describes how the author's decision to include the excerpts from her psychiatric reports was initially viewed as 'an advertisement for whichever idea you had of Joan Didion, either that she was bravely exposing what others might work hard to conceal, or that she was an exhibitionist'.

A good deal of this variety also comes down to the space that Didion's chosen form—with its collage of fragments and list-like logic—leaves for readerly interpretation. I have not always loved Didion's work as much as a person who came of age when and where I did might be expected to—I was, for one thing, thoroughly flummoxed by *Slouching Towards Bethlehem* when I first read it in my early twenties. I can also see how the ambiguous tone of her writing from this period might risk suggesting, implicitly or explicitly, that because Didion tells us she has failed to find cohesive meaning in what she's describing, she's not doing the inevitable work of interpreting and filtering and constructing all of the detail she presents, as the significant blind spots identified in her work by writers such as Castillo and Mariah Rigg illustrate. I note, too, that—as Jay Caspian Kang observes—'Didion herself eventually grew wary of her own ambiguity', with much of her later writing adopting a more direct style.

But I have come to admire Didion's willingness, in 'The White Album', to resist making meaning transparent. To allow things to stand in a place of uncertainty and leave space for interpretation; invite it in, even—a quality that strikes me as key to the continuing appeal of this era of her work to many readers. I admire it partly because I recognise something like the opposite in myself: a need to pin things down, to be certain of their significance. Back when I was making those lists—of things to pack, and things to remember—I was also working as a journalist, and one of the main aims of my professional life was to ensure my meaning was as clear as possible; one of my eventual frustrations with journalistic writing was that I couldn't work out how to make it reflect the contradictions and uncertainties I often observed and experienced. There seemed to be too great a distance between the pose of confident authority such writing seemed to require of me, and the unsure, unsettled self who existed off the page.

o o o

For some years, I maintained the habit of writing expansive lists of new year's resolutions on my computer each January. The longest had forty-nine separate items. I will not reproduce all or even most of them here—that seems excessively solipsistic, even for me; besides which, they're not very interesting—but one thing that has struck me is how strict and specific they often were.

Do 12 km fun run in May

Write six short stories

Read for at least half an hour each day

Write one essay each month

Floss twice daily

Here is what I see when I read these lists back today: I see the person who wrote them, and how hard she is trying. I see the ways that mental illness has made her self-absorbed, in the sense that her own unhappiness and the ways she might address it and the ways she has tried to distract herself from it have soaked up so much of her attention and energy. I see the person who wrote these long lists of resolutions; the teenager reading her star sign; the girl in her witchy phase, hoping she might be able to see what's coming. A writer, trying to wrestle some sense from experience—trying to find a form that fits the sense of internal disorder she has known.

In the way these lists repeat one another, with their similar-but-different headings and line items, I also see something of Didion and her drawer full of licence-plate numbers. Something of the ritual, or the incantation. I see that I was never going to stick to all of these resolutions; I couldn't bring myself to floss more than once a day, never mind the other stuff. But I found something soothing in the repetition of them; in imagining the possibility of a future self who might do all of these things, no matter how likely or unlikely it was she might come to exist.

I no longer make new year's resolutions, or believe I have psychic powers, or read my horoscope in magazines. But, as I was writing this essay, I was planning a trip to Melbourne to visit family; my first outside the state in some years, due to Covid. I knew the weather would be unpredictable, and worried about having the right clothes for the conditions. And so I opened the app on my phone, and started packing my suitcase again.

Coda

Around the time I was beginning to think I might be finished with these essays—could finally draw a line, even a faint one, under the project of processing what all of these things have meant to me—an auction house in New York State announced it would sell off hundreds of Joan Didion's possessions. She had died, nearly a year earlier, at the age of eighty-seven. I was also, around this time, beginning to realise the folly of trying to write about someone as extensively discussed as Didion, given not only the longevity of her life and career but also the broad array of what she has meant to people: there was no singular Didion to write about. Even so, on reading the news, it felt like that awkward moment when you're talking about someone right as they walk into a room.

Discussion of the auction quickly lit up my writing-friends group chat. We clicked through the online catalogue and engaged in spirited but entirely hypothetical discussions about which of the lots we'd buy, given the disposable funds. One friend fancied the oversized faux-tortoiseshell sunglasses that were somewhat similar to the ones Didion had worn, aged eighty, in an advertising campaign for the luxury fashion house Celine. Another was drawn to the romance, the sense of possibility, that might come with obtaining her writing desk or one of the bulk lots of her unused notebooks. I liked the look of a blue-and-white porcelain plate printed with California tourist attractions (redwood forests, Hollywood, Yosemite Falls), and a photorealist print of the ocean, and the famous black-and-white photograph of Didion standing by her Corvette Stingray, wearing a long dress and sandals.

This image was the Didion reflected in media coverage of the auction, much of which focused on these objects as irrefutable evidence of her ineffable, understated elegance (the battered Le Creuset cookware! The cashmere throws! Those sunglasses!). And yet many of the lots struck me as almost comical in their *lack* of glamour. The white slipcovered sofa—complete 'with minor tears and staining'—appeared almost identical to one of the pair my mum has owned since the late '90s (she would never forgive me if I didn't add that hers are wholly intact and spotlessly clean at all times). A glass paperweight with a monogrammed 'J' looked like the kind of thing you might receive as a going-away gift from a job you never really liked, but then keep only out of a sense of misplaced obligation. There was a black apron, printed with the words, 'Maybe broccoli doesn't like you either'. A copy of Ottolenghi's *Plenty*. A faded box of ballpoint pens. A small handful of buttons, and a pair of stainless-steel scissors with a faux-tortoiseshell handle, perhaps to match the sunglasses.

As much as I wanted to feel above it all, I decided I wouldn't mind owning those scissors. But what really snagged my attention was Lot 50, a group of seashells and beach pebbles accompanied by a photograph of them arranged alongside decanters and small sculptures and other odds and ends on Didion's fireplace mantle. They were listed with a guide price of US$100–200.

o o o

I suppose I was intrigued by the seashells in part because I already had a similar collection of my own, although I can't imagine they'd be worth more than a dollar or two. They're scattered around the room where I work, mixed in with a tiny figurine of a cat, a small crocodile made from glass, a plastic squirrel that I bought at a famous cowboy-boot shop in Texas, and shards of coloured glass worn smooth by the sea.

One of my pebbles came from a place where, on a windless late-winter afternoon, the water was like glass and the sand almost painfully cold underfoot. Where I'd walked carefully over the rocks that wrapped the headland in a collar. And it was somewhere around there, in one of the small bays fringed with a green lace of leaves, that I'd stopped, out of sight of the surfers at the main beach, and tossed my dad's ashes—or a portion of them; the volume had been so much greater than I'd expected—into the ocean. First, they sat slick and grey on the surface; then they broke apart in the churn of the swell. And, as they dissipated into the ocean, I stooped to collect the first shard of rock that came to hand.

Contemplating my little collection led me to thinking about how I know that one of these pebbles is *the* pebble, even if I can't remember which. There are four contenders. A small, roundish stone with a lightly dimpled surface of mottled white, cream and very light grey. One that's slightly larger and smoother, on which a chalky white coating has partly rubbed away to reveal a dark grey interior. A chunk of creamy quartz whose surface is striated with cracks and small fissures stained reddish. And the smallest, almost black, with a pitted texture, which leaves behind scant grains of white sand whenever it is placed atop a table.

(The latter, with its trail of grit, always reminds me of Natasha Sholl's words about grief: how it is not contained; how it leaks on everything.)

o o o

If a lot of the items in Didion's auction seemed almost pedestrian, then there were also plenty of reminders that these were not any ordinary eighty-seven-year-old woman's possessions. It wasn't only that there were artworks by Richard Serra and Robert Rauschenberg and Cy Twombly and Ed Ruscha, but that one of the Ruscha lithographs was accompanied by a note of thanks, signed by the artist. And it wasn't just that there were photographs by Annie Leibovitz and Patti Smith, but that the photographs by Leibovitz were of Didion and her daughter, Quintana Roo, and that the pictures by Smith bore personal dedications in a spidery script.

All of this extraordinariness was reflected in the bids that people eventually placed. Although the initial guide prices had been tantalisingly affordable, they quite predictably blew out. It had been estimated, for instance, that the three lots of notebooks would each go for somewhere between US$100–200; they eventually fetched a minimum of US$9000 apiece. Two liberally stained leather bins sold for US$5500; the Celine sunglasses a genuinely quite astonishing US$27,000. The seashells I'd coveted topped out at seven grand. Given the auction was raising funds for worthy causes—for Parkinson's care and research, and for scholarships for women writers in Didion's hometown of Sacramento—this was undoubtedly good news.

And yet, something about it made me uneasy. And it took Lot 26, the ebony-inlaid mahogany table ('Expected nicks to the legs. Structurally sound') at which Didion's husband, the writer John Gregory Dunne, had suffered a fatal heart attack, to make me realise what. Even though it sold for a bit more than US$4000, somehow that didn't seem nearly enough.

o o o

In an essay about Didion's auction, writer Hannah Gold found herself particularly taken with two pieces of well-used cookware, each of them liberally scorched and stained by years of use. She thought the listing's disclaimer—that the items were to be sold 'as is', marks and all—quite funny, 'as though Joan Didion's detritus, the remnants from her cooking, weren't the point'. To this end, Gold quoted a rare-book dealer named Arthur Fournier, who endeavoured to explain the allure of objects such as these with reference to the anthropological concept of 'contagion magic', which suggests that things which have been in contact with one another continue to be linked in some way even after they're separated. (This is the basis, for example, for witches requiring a lock of someone's hair to cast a spell against them.) 'What is the market price of magic?' Gold asked rhetorically.

Many of the articles written in the lead up to and aftermath of the auction suggested that bidding on Didion's possessions, or going to see them displayed at the auction house in New York State—or even just browsing through the online catalogue, as my friends and I did—was a way to feel close to a woman known to us in life in ways that were no less meaningful for being partial; that is, through her work and her public image. And yet, there also seemed to be a palpable sense of absence to this stuff. The auction included aprons and glasses, but no actual clothing. There were the empty notebooks and themed bundles of various books ('Books about California'; 'Women Poets'), but no scribbled-in pages; no paperbacks bearing Didion's annotations (such material was headed for an official joint archive dedicated to her and Dunne's work). Didion the person was present in this stuff, but she was also—in ways obvious and less so—absent.

o o o

Another thing happened around the time I thought I was finished with these essays: a copy of my dad's medical records, which I'd requested some time earlier, finally arrived. When I found the thick packet of paper amid a scant pile of parcels on my front verandah one morning, I was eager to open the envelope. I guess I'd thought the records might help me check some of the timeline and facts related to the stories I have told here. I hadn't considered how they might make me feel.

I quickly found that most of the material inside didn't make a lot of sense to me. The photocopied forms and charts were filled with hospital jargon and unfamiliar acronyms, all inscribed in the unde-cipherable handwriting of medical stereotype. But then I came to a more orderly entry, written by one of the nurses, relating to a conversation with my dad about his state of mind in the wake of his diagnosis. According to the notes, he was having difficulty accepting what was happening, and didn't like to be left alone. The nurse wrote that they had sat with him, talking all of this over, for quite a while.

Reading all of this made me think—thoughts cascading, by association—of the first time I'd gone to visit Dad in hospital. How I had been unable to stop sobbing when I'd seen him hooked up to the machines. How he'd also ended up in tears; the first time I'd seen him cry. Of another visit, when I'd failed to recognise him lying in the back of the ambulance in the hospital carpark because he had looked so thin and old and unwell—so much like someone who was dying. Of my final visit, when a nurse had come down to find me in the hospital canteen, where I was eating a sandwich (I don't remember what kind). How she'd said, 'I think he waited until you were gone.'

They also made me think of a particular picture I have of him, which I tend to keep out of sight in my attic. It's a black-and-white portrait, head and shoulders, a serious sort of semi-smile on his face that I can only imagine was a touch ironic. It was taken for work, but was also the picture we printed out and framed to sit on top of his coffin at his funeral. I can't remember why we chose it—that whole time appears ever-blurrier at it retreats into hindsight. I suppose I ended up with it for the same reason I have all the rest of his stuff.

I've never really liked this photo. Something about it feels so formal, even clinical; I know he would have felt uncomfortable posing for it (an aversion to having my picture taken is another thing I have inherited from him). Perhaps because my perception of this picture is dominated by my dad's apparent lack of ease, it has, over the years, become a stand-in for the pieces of him for which no other material representation exists. I have no physical reminders of his depression, of the day he moved out of our home, of his time in the hospital, of the times he was impatient, or absent, or sad—so instead my knowledge of them, and my scant memories of such moments, became concentrated in this somewhat generic but otherwise blameless black-and-white portrait. It had soaked them up, kept them quarantined, contained.

But then I'd opened that packet of medical records, and those other pieces of the person I knew had come spilling out, and I found I was unable to set them aside.

o o o

In her latter decades, Didion came to be associated as much with grief as with glamour, following the publication of *The Year of Magical Thinking* and then *Blue Nights*, about the deaths of John and Quintana respectively. In the former book, she writes about how quickly 'the ordinary instant' can morph into 'sudden disaster'; about being unable to get rid of her husband's shoes, 'because he would need shoes if he was to return'. She also writes about something I instantly recognised, which she calls 'the vortex effect': the way a seemingly benign scene or object or path of thought could, in grief, quickly suck her into previously happy memories rendered newly painful by circumstance.

By some similar effect, as I was reading about the auction of Didion's possessions, I made a connection between the careful sifting of the contents of her home that it and the curation of her archive would have entailed to the parallel process my stepmum and I had undertaken at her house in England all those years ago. The two shared some things in common: recall that the books and sheaves of paper which bore my dad's handwriting took on special significance for me, just as the annotated books did for the curators of Didion's archive. But mostly they were quite different endeavours, in which the assessments of each item were made according to quite different criteria.

This confluence of divergence and similarity also reminded me of how, the morning after Dad died, I'd been irrationally bereft to unroll the newspaper—this was back when almost everyone still got it delivered, wrapped tightly in plastic—to find no mention of his passing on the front page or page two or three or on any of the others. (Later, there was a funeral notice, and some well wishes from friends and family in the death notices, but we had, of course, paid for those to be printed.) It was funny—funny is not the word—because it wasn't that I had actually expected my father's death to make the news: he was not a famous or high-profile person. Rather, I was experiencing what writer and artist Vanessa Berry describes as 'one of the confounding aspects of grief ... the contrast between the pain of loss, acute and interior and lonely, with the oblivious churn of life as it continues all around'.

I often think of this when a very famous person dies, and their family releases a statement thanking the public for their well wishes and asking for privacy at this difficult time. I can understand the request—of course they don't want to be hounded while they are sad and low—but I also feel slightly jealous (again, I'm not sure this is the right word). What is happening to them has, at least, been acknowledged on a scale that might come close to feeling commensurate with their loss. The world—or at least a good slice of it—is grieving with them. Indeed, Didion's nephew, Griffin Dunne, mentioned this in his own statement after Didion's death: 'Now I find myself in grief, which I share with so many others'. (It had not yet occurred to me that there might be other reasons a death could end up in the news; take the example of novelist Brooke Davis, whose mother, she writes, made 'the front page of the newspaper for all the wrong reasons: Freak Gate Crush Death in capitals'.)

However, if the person you have lost is an ordinary person who has died an unremarkable death—certainly not the right words—then you have to find a way to accommodate the loss amid the churn.

o o o

I suppose that my row of four pebbles might be considered failures as mnemonic objects, given that I do not know which one is *the* pebble. Most of the rest of my collection of seashells and sea glass and little rocks have similarly lost their specificity. A few are distinctive enough to maintain a firm link to a particular place in my mind; of the remainder, I can say only that some are from beaches relatively near to my house and others are from further away.

I am not entirely sure this matters. I did toy, for a while, with the idea of working out which pebble was *the* pebble; figured I could visit the beach where I'd scattered Dad's ashes—it's near the small town where my mum lives—to see which of the little rocks was the best match for the boulders I found there. Maybe I could ask a geologist—I know a few of them, because of my dad—which looked most likely to have come from that place. I thought Dad would have quite liked that; me finally showing an interest in this thing he had loved.

In the end, I didn't do any of that. Instead, I was reminded of another rock: the memorial we paid to have placed at a cemetery not far from my house in the months after my dad's death. I'm unsure where I got the idea to do so, but I recall being accompanied by Mum to a small office where I chose from a catalogue an option for a large piece of granite, to be adorned with a brass plaque and then installed in the cemetery's rose garden. Given Dad's profession, it seemed the only option. Plus, the woman at the cemetery told us we could inter another lot of his ashes beside its base, which we later did at a small and somewhat makeshift ceremony attended by a bunch of my dad's geologist friends. (They were all very complimentary about the granite.)

At the time, organising all of this was intensely important to me. But in the years since, I have visited the cemetery maybe no more than a dozen times. I would not interpret this as a failure, however, either on my part or the memorial's. Indeed, it strikes me as an indication that it has been working as intended. 'Once a grave has been marked, you can visit it, but you do not have to,' writes Lewis Hyde in *A Primer for Forgetting*. It has been enough to know that it is there.

o o o

When my dad died, I was twenty and he was ten days away from turning fifty-eight. I have been trying to write about him, and how it has felt to grieve him, for nearly half my life. The dust that accumulates on the pebbles and the frames of the photographs of him and the other things connected to him on my shelves reminds me of how much time has passed.

It also reminds me of a phenomenon I learnt about when I was an undergraduate studying Italian. We were told about how, oftentimes, the image migrants retain of their homeland is one rooted in the moment of their departure. For this reason, returning could be difficult, given the disjunct between the place they remember and the ways it has inevitably evolved in their absence. A kind of mourning might occur for this past—idealised or otherwise—that they may well have held precious for many years.

Something similar would have happened with my dad, and with me, had he lived. I would have changed, as would have he, in ways that would have been good and bad and perhaps a bit of both. Either way, the loss of those possibilities has also felt like a kind of grief.

o o o

I find myself, now, no closer to an ending. The example of the auction of Didion's stuff and my dad's medical records and the cascade or vortex—or whatever you want to call it—of thoughts and memories they've brought forth illustrate the difficulties of that. Those seashells and rocks and strangely un-scribbled-in books have suggested that I cannot relegate any of this definitively to the past. That though Didion urges us, towards the end of *Magical Thinking*, to 'relinquish the dead, let them go, keep them dead'—to 'let them become the photograph on the table'; 'let go of them in the water'—their lives will continue to be intertwined with ours in unpredictable and often unexpected ways. (Grief gets on everything.)

As I write this, my eye falls on yet another picture of my dad; one that I keep in a frame in a place on my desk where I see it every day. It's of a man wearing jeans and a checked shirt, his arm around his daughter's shoulders. They're on holiday, their backs to the camera as they walk out of the frame. I can't see the expressions on their faces, but their strides look to be almost in sync.

Notes on sources

Edward Sylvester Hynes

Jane Bennett's discussion of hoarding comes from her presentation, 'Powers of the Hoard: Artistry and Agency in a World of Vibrant Matter', from 13 September 2011 at the Vera List Center in New York City (https://veralistcenter.org/events/jane-bennett-powers-of-the-hoard-artistry-and-agency-in-a-world-of-vibrant-matter/). Max Black's book on metaphor is *Models and Metaphors: Studies in Language and Philosophy* (Cornell University Press, 1962). The details on Edward Sylvester Hynes' life are drawn largely from Mark Bryant's *Dictionary of Twentieth-Century British Cartoonists and Caricaturists* (Routledge, 2018).

Baby Teeth

This essay references the novels *Jane Eyre* (1847) and *Villette* (1853) by Charlotte Bronte, *Wuthering Heights* (1847) by Emily Bronte, *The Picture of Dorian Gray* (1891) by Oscar Wilde, *Wide Sargasso Sea* (1966) by Jean Rhys, *Little Women* (1868–9) by Louisa May Alcott, and *The Mill on the Floss* (1860) by George Eliot, along with the novella 'The Yellow Wallpaper' (1892) by Charlotte Perkins Gilman. It also refers to Susan Stewart's 'Reading a Drawer', from the journal *Room One Thousand* (2014); Deborah Lutz's 'The Dead Still Among Us: Victorian Secular Relics, Hair Jewelry, and Death Culture', from the journal *Victorian Literature and Culture* (2011); and Melissa Febos's essay collection *Girlhood* (Bloomsbury, 2021). My thinking in this essay was also influenced by reading David Lowenthal's *The Past is a Foreign Country* and Svetlana Boym's *The Future of Nostalgia*, among other books. For background information on the significance of abalone fishing to the Perth Chinese community and on the twentieth-century reputation of the Blue Hole respectively, I'm grateful to Li Chen's 2017 PhD thesis from Edith Cowan University, titled 'Chinese diaspora and Western Australian nature (Perth region): A study of material engagement with the natural world in diasporic culture', and the National Library of Australia's Trove for access to digitised historical newspaper articles from the Perth *Daily News*, *The West Australian*, *The Western Mail* and the Perth *Mirror*.

The Things We Live With, Part I

This essay references Sarah Manguso's books *Ongoingness* (Graywolf Press, 2015) and *300 Arguments* (Graywolf Press, 2017), along with Alain de Botton's *The Art of Travel* (Penguin, 2003). It also refers to Beverly Gordon's journal article 'The Souvenir: Messenger of the Extraordinary' from the *Journal of Popular Culture* (1986) and Mark Halliday's 'Relentless Whoosh: Poetry of Ongoingness' from *The Hopkins Review* (2020). The quote by Paul Theroux paraphrases a line from *Dark Star Safari* (Penguin, 2003). For background information on the impact of bias in the treatment of pain (and in healthcare more generally), I'm grateful to the work of researchers including Janice A. Sabin and Anke Samulowitz, among many others.

A Small, Brown Suitcase

This essay references *Camera Lucida* by Roland Barthes (Hill and Wang, 1981). The quote by Lulah Ellender is from the essay 'Finding Lives between the Lines' from the journal *a/b: Auto/Biography Studies* (2020).

Dear Lucy

Peter Turchi's book is *Maps of the Imagination* (Trinity University Press, 2007). 'Holidays with Men' is from *Blueberries* by Ellena Savage

(Text, 2020). Chet van Duzer's comments are from his presentation titled '"With Savage Pictures Fill Their Gaps": On Cartographers' Fear of Blank Spaces', from 15 November 2017 at the New York Map Society (https://www.youtube.com/watch?v=Dg5UUGzossI). 'On Exactitude in Science' is from *Collected Fictions* by Jorge Luis Borges, translated by Andrew Hurley (Penguin, 1999).

The Things We Live With, Part II

This essay's epigraph is from 'Home and Homelessness' by Kim Dovey, from the book *Home Environments*, edited by Irwin Altman and Carol M. Werner (Springer, 1985). It also references Maria Papas's journal article 'Incoherence/coherence in narratives of illness or trauma: On the necessity of challenging conventional narrative structures' from *TEXT* (2020); *Smile or Die* by Barbara Ehrenreich (Granta, 2010); Lucia Osborne-Crowley's essay 'What if we never recover?' from *Meanjin* (2021); and *Small Acts of Disappearance* by Fiona Wright (Giramondo, 2015). (I'm also grateful to Wright for inspiring, among other things, the format of these notes on sources.)

On We Go

This essay references *Mrs P's Journey* by Sarah Hartley (Simon and Schuster, 2017), along with Phyllis Pearsall's own books, *From Bedsitter to Household Name* (Geographers' A-Z Map Company, 1990) and *Fleet Street, Tite Street, Queer Street* (self-published, 1983), and *A Field Guide to Getting Lost*, by Rebecca Solnit (Canongate, 2017). Pearsall's half-brother, Alex Gross, has written extensively about her and the A-Z at untoldsixties.net/a_to_z.htm. London writers Peter Berthoud and Peter Watts have also discussed the controversy of the A-Z origin story at peterberthoud.co.uk and greatwen.com respectively. The quoted interview with Pearsall aired on the BBC Woman's Hour on 7 November 1984. The quote in the final line is drawn from Sarah Lyall's obituary of Pearsall in the *New York Times* (1996).

Via del Paradiso

This essay references Carl Phillips' essay 'On Restlessness' from the *New England Review* (2009). The quote from Susan Stewart is from *On Longing: Narratives of the Miniature, the Gigantic, the Souvenir, the Collection* (Duke University Press, 1993); the Virginia Woolf line is from her essay 'The Humane Art', from *The Death of the Moth and Other Essays* (Hogarth Press, 1942).

Swimming, or Hoping

This essay references Joan Didion's essay 'The White Album', from her collection of the same name (Simon and Schuster, 1979), along with the preface and the essays 'Letter from Paradise, 21° 19' N., 157° 52' W' and 'On Keeping A Notebook' from *Slouching Towards Bethlehem* (Farrar, Straus and Giroux, 1968). It also refers to the following writing about Didion: 'Joan Didion and the Voice of America' by Hilton Als, from *The New Yorker* (2021); 'Main Character Syndrome' by Elaine Castillo, from her book *How to Read Now* (Atlantic, 2022); 'A Fraying Narrative' by Emily Carmichael, from *The Believer* (2022); 'Reporting Nuclear Dread: The Stranger at Didion's Door' by Franny Nudelman, from *a/b: Auto/Biography Studies* (2016); 'Joan Didion's Magic Trick' by Caitlin Flanagan, from *The Atlantic* (2022); 'Notes from a Haole Settler: Reading Joan Didion Taught Me How to Not Write about Hawai'i' by Mariah Rigg, from *Catapult* (2022); and 'I've Spent 25 Years as a Joan Didion Thief' by Jay Caspian Kang, from *The New York Times* (2021). The quote about patriarchal structures of thought is from Laura Julier's 1988 PhD thesis from the University of Iowa, titled 'We tell ourselves stories in order to live: Patriarchal fictions and the narrative essays of Joan Didion'.

The discussion about lists refers to 'The Potential and Limitations of Studying Lists' by Lucie Doležalová, from her edited book *The Charm of a List* (Cambridge Scholars Publishing, 2009); 'List as Form' by Sasha Su-Ling Welland, from *Writing Anthropology: Essays on Craft and Commitment*, edited by Carole McGranahan (Duke University

Press, 2020); Lulah Ellender's aforementioned 'Finding Lives between the Lines'; and 'The Literary List: A Survey of its Uses and Deployments' by Robert Belknap, from *Literary Imagination: The Review of the Association of Literary Scholars and Critics* (2000). The information of schema therapy is from *Schema Therapy: A Practitioner's Guide* by Jeffrey E. Young, Janet S. Klosko and Marjorie E. Weishaar (The Guildford Press, 2003), and the quote from Sanah Ahsan is from her September 2022 article in *The Guardian* titled 'I'm a psychologist – and I believe we've been told devastating lies about mental health'. The discussion of memory references Penelope Lively's *Ammonites and Leaping Fish* (Penguin, 2013); Charles Fernyhough's *Pieces of Light* (Profile Books, 2012); Lewis Hyde's *A Primer for Forgetting* (Farrar, Straus and Giroux, 2019); Douwe Draaisma's *Forgetting: Myths, Perils and Compensations* (Yale University Press, 2015); and Edmund de Waal's *The Hare with Amber Eyes* (Farrar, Straus and Giroux, 2010). Brian Dillon's *Essayism* (Fitzcarraldo Editions, 2017) is referenced throughout.

Coda

The auction 'An American Icon: Property from the Collection of Joan Didion' was conducted by Stair Galleries in Hudson, New York, on 16 November 2022. This essay also references Didion's memoirs *The Year of Magical Thinking* (Knopf, 2005) and *Blue Nights* (Knopf, 2011), along with Natasha Sholl's *Found, Wanting* (Ultimo, 2022); 'Goodbye to All That' by Hannah Gold, from *The Baffler* (2022); Vanessa Berry's essay 'Fly Away Bird', from her collection *Gentle and Fierce* (Giramondo, 2021); 'Catching the light: Finding words for grief with Lewis, Didion and Woolf' by Brooke Davis, from *TEXT* journal; and Lewis Hyde's aforementioned *A Primer for Forgetting*.

Acknowledgements

This book was written on Whadjuk Noongar Boodja, where I am fortunate to live and work. I also spent short but meaningful periods working on this project on the lands of the Bibulmun and Minang peoples of the Noongar nation, and on the lands of the Darug and the Gundungurra peoples. I pay my respects to their Elders, past and present. Sovereignty was never ceded.

This book started life as part of my PhD thesis at the University of Western Australia. During that time, my work was supported financially by an Australian Government Research Training Program (RTP) Scholarship and in all other ways by Tanya Dalziell and Daniel Juckes. Working with the two of them has been one of the greatest joys of my professional life so far, and I'm deeply grateful for their kindness, intelligence, patience and friendship. At UWA and within academia generally, I'd also like to thank to Kate Noske, Sharen Bart, Charli Newton, Marina Deller and my officemates, particularly Sarah Yeung and Anna Quercia-Thomas. Thank you, most especially, to Angela Italiano for her unwavering belief in me and in this project.

While working on these essays, I spent time at the Katharine Susannah Prichard Writers' Centre as an Invited Writer-in-Residence, and at Varuna the National Writer's House on an Invited Residency, the latter supported by the Department of Local Government, Sport and Cultural Industries (DLGSC) Culture and the Arts (WA) Arts U-15k grant scheme. An earlier version of my essay 'A Small, Brown Suitcase' was published as 'The Point of the Thing' in *AXON*: Creative Explorations 11.2. A version of 'On We Go' was shortlisted in the 2022 AAWP-*Westerly* Life Writing Prize. Thank you to each of these organisations, programs and publications for their support.

My publisher, Terri-ann White, saw potential in these essays when they were barely half formed. I am intensely grateful for the opportunities she has given me, and for her expertise, dedication and advocacy. Big thanks to Nadine Davidoff for her sensitive editorial guidance, and to Becky Chilcott of Chil3 and The Pattern Hunters for making my wildest cover dreams come true.

Thank you to all the members of the Western Australian and Australian writing and literary communities who have welcomed me so warmly into their ranks. Special thanks in particular to Sam Carmody, Alaina Gougoulis, Karys McEwen, Jen Pinkerton and Stephen Scourfield for their generous early advice. Thank you to Stephen and Niall McIlroy for being my first, formative writing community and to Niall for his keen eye. Thank you to Will Yeoman for his friendship and encouragement over many years. Special thanks to 'Lucy' and to the many wonderful friends who have cheered me along. A massive shoutout, and eternal gratitude, to The Lads, my adored writing family.

It is an unlucky fate for any family to have a life writer in their midst, and I'm extremely fortunate to have the love and support of mine: Christina, Nathan, Zoe, Eleanor, Jess and Fred; the Mazzoni clan (special thanks to Bruno and Kate for taking such good care of me in Sydney); and the extended Craddock and Biondillo families. I'm very grateful to my stepmum Lynn for her generosity and understanding, and to Aunty Joan for all of her love and care. Thank you, most especially, to my mother Diana, who read this book three times before it had even been typeset. She holds all of us together, always.

If it is an unlucky fate to have a life writer in the family, it is a special misfortune to have one for a partner. I'm immensely grateful to my husband, David, not only for his encouragement and understanding throughout the course of writing these essays, but also for supporting me through so many of the personal difficulties they describe. Thank you, too, to the other member of our little family: our dog Pickle, who has been literally by my side throughout most of this work.

Finally, I dedicate this book to the memory of my late father, Dr Bruce Nisbet.

About Upswell

Upswell Publishing was established in 2021 by Terri-ann White as a not-for-profit press. A perceived gap in the market for distinctive literary works in fiction, poetry and narrative non-fiction was the motivation. In her years as a bookseller, writer and then publisher, Terri-ann has maintained a watch on literary books and the way they insinuate themselves into a cultural space and are then located within our literary and cultural inheritance. She is interested in making books to last: books with the potential to still be noticed, and noted, after decades and thus be ripe to influence new literary histories.

About this typeface

Book designer Becky Chilcott chose
Foundry Origin not only as a strong,
carefully considered, and dependable
typeface, but also to honour her late
friend and mentor, type designer Freda
Sack, who oversaw the project. Designed
by Freda's long-standing colleague,
Stuart de Rozario, much like Upswell
Publishing, Foundry Origin was created
out of the desire to say something new.